Elana R.

you are greatly Appreciated
thank you for everything!

Expect Great Thing To Happen

Richard D. Marks

"Richard Marks has done an excellent job capturing the fundamental characteristics of the finest business people. He understands that if you want to be highly effective at anything, your journey begins on the inside. This book is full of insights, inspirational stories, and vital information you can use right away to make great things happen. Buy it, read it, and put its wisdom into practice!"

— Ken Blanchard, coauthor of The New One Minute Manager® and Simple Truths of Leadership: 52 Ways to Be a Servant Leader and Build Trust

"The author vulnerably shares details of his personal journey that will encourage others who may doubt they have the credentials to achieve their dreams and goals. Our business culture has emphasized one path as the only way to reach your goals and realize your dreams, but Richard shows that alternative paths can prevail if the individual persists! Read it and Expect Great Things to Happen!"

— Dr. Lisa M Greene, Optometrist, practice consultant and speaker Asheville Vision & Wellness

"Richard has done a terrific job identifying the five key practices that support leaders in performing at their optimal best level: Self-Awareness, Self-Confidence, Motivation, Self-Discipline, and Emotional Intelligence. These skills, when intentionally practiced together, will have a significantly positive impact in your personal as well as your professional life. Expect Great Things to Happen is a must read!"!

— Gregg Ward, Author of the best-selling, award-winning business fable, "The Respectful Leader"

"An outstanding must-read self-help book for those who want to experience an exciting career and life journey by starting from within yourself and understanding how to connect with others with passion. By putting Mr. Mark's Principles into practice, the readers are sure to become better leaders, communicators, listeners, and motivators. You will immediately be driven to be better in all areas of your life."

— Angela Grove, Workforce Development Leader within the federal government.

"Richard takes the reader on a self-explorative journey towards self-awareness. In today's culture we are bombarded by so much false and sensationalized information which can take a toll on a person's psyche. The power of this book is the reader will be empowered to embrace their own skills, talents and abilities and not live life under someone else's expectation or perception. This book touches upon many issues that people are struggling with; spirituality, self-worth, self-esteem, self-confidence and negative mindset. Personally, I have struggled with all of these PLUS more. Richard did an exceptional job in addressing these issues and the best way to address them and overcome them. This is a must read for personal AND professional growth and advancement."

— Tanya Brown M.A. Speaker, Life Empowerment Coach and the youngest sister of the late Nicole Brown Simpson

EXPECT GREAT THINGS TO HAPPEN

EXPECT GREAT THINGS TO HAPPEN

Five Core Principles of Highly Effective Business Professionals

Richard D. Marks

JONES MEDIA
PUBLISHING

DEDICATION

This book is dedicated to all the people who have been negatively impacted by their leaders. It can serve as a blueprint for a better understanding of your experiences with these individuals.

It's also dedicated to business leaders and professionals who are seeking direction, self-improvement, and those who want to have a positive impact on their spheres of influence.

CONTENTS

ACKNOWLEDGEMENTS

I would like to acknowledge the book *Emotional Intelligence* and its author, Travis Bradberry. In *Emotional Intelligence*, Bradberry lays out a simple blueprint for cultivating one's emotional intelligence, breaking it down into four categories which I will reference throughout this book: Self-Awareness, Self-Management, Social Awareness, and Social Skills.

I would like to thank Art Barter for taking the time to sit with me, encouraging me to write this book. You let me know that if I'm going to be serious about this business – as a trainer, coach, speaker, and author – that a book should be in my immediate future.

I would like to thank Ken Blanchard for setting the example of having a global business that teaches leaders how to lead, to invest in others, and impact lives positively.

Thank you, Jeremy Jones of Jones Media Publishing, for your strategies and processes on how to write a book. I would like to thank Laurie Lamson for your awesome editing skills, helping me bring this book to life.

I would like to thank my wife Eleasa for her words of encouragement and support. My mother Reeda for always reminding me to put God first in all that I do. My dad, "Eddie Jordan" (RIP), for teaching me how to love unconditionally. My beloved grandparents, Clarence and Cletuis Marks, Joe and Mama Jordan for teaching me kindness– even when life appears to be unfair.

To my handsome sons, Ricardo and Richard, for being awesome husbands, fathers, and men of great integrity. To my beautiful daughters, Devan, Elexis, and Evana, for being brave in pursuing their goals and objectives in life.

To my granddaughters, Maggie, Aviana, Violet, and Penelope, for bringing unlimited smiles and joy into my heart and into the world.

To my aunties, Dafine, Freda, Catherine, and Sue, thank you for being smart and courageous women, still standing strong and beating the odds.

To my Uncle Gary, thank you for your meekness and service to our country. Thank you, Uncle Chink (RIP), for your sense of humor and your brotherly love shared with my daddy.

To my brother, Christopher, thank you for always being there. Thank you for positively challenging me and your strategic-creative thinking. Thank you for not ever giving up and being a dad whom I admire. To my wonderful and beautiful sister, Diana. Thank you for always caring and being unafraid to speak your mind and stand up for the truth. Dad would be so proud of you.

To Brandon and Rondalyn, I love you both. Your mom, Sherly, always showed me warmth and kindness, may she rest in peace.

To Virginia, my stepmother, thank you for encouraging me to be my best and to eat my vegetables. To Gan-Gan, for being a pioneer in education and believing in the goodness of mankind.

To Bradie Davis, for blessing me with our son, Ricardo, and to Vanessa Moncrief, thank you for our children, Devan and Richard.

To my cousins Donna, Ray, Derick, and Dale Lamar, thank you for the fun summers and great memories.

To my first double cousins, Jeff and Scott Gipson, for the sleepovers as kids and the joy of Cocoa Pebbles in the mornings. To your wonder mom, Jenetta, for loving me as one of her own.

Thank you to the Harris Family for being positive role models: Jenny, DaRhonda, Kieth, Lisa (RIP), James, Vick, and Hayward, aka Dynamite.

Great Auntie Lorine and Uncle Willie James (RIP), thank you for your love and introducing me to fried fish.

Mark Norman aka "Sweet Honey-Bun Under the Sun," thank you for keeping it real with me.

I would like to thank the U.S. Army for planting those seeds of discipline in me at an early age. You taught me to value my skills and talents. Though the lessons were TOUGH, I learned to trust myself and to take a chance on me.

I would also like to thank my "Nextel" crew: Walter Hinkle, John Moriarty, Fred Hamilton, Chuck Beare, Chuck Buzan, and JT Cole. You were positive and instrumental leaders who took a chance on me. Those experiences were instrumental in the collection of stories in this book.

I would like to thank the crew from MCI. For those experiences good, bad, and different really shaped me into the type of responsible leader I am today.

I would like to take the time to acknowledge the fine folks I had the opportunity to work with at Cricket Wireless. Annette Jacobs, for demonstrating the characteristics of a very thoughtful and caring, yet strategic leader, who knew how to get the job done. I would like to thank Randy Newman for giving me a chance and challenging me positively to be strategic and tactical in my execution, and for being a great friend. Also, Joe Zeccola and Melody Zorgdrager for my Albuquerque and El Paso experiences.

I would like to thank my fellow peer group while working for Cricket: Stephanie Fortuna, Briana Jolicoeur, Liz Faraimo, Milica Pugh, Jason Beiter, Marlon Young – my business "partners in crime." Collectively we did so much for the betterment of the organization and the people we led. Thank you so much for your kindness, the funny times, and the memorable experiences I will always carry with me. You guys are forever rockstars.

I would like to thank some of my high school friends who are still knocking it out of the park. Johnny Shelton, Sterling Marshall, Ralph Jefferson, Pastor Ronnie Webb, and Dr. Sandra Jackson, you folks have always led by example and challenged me positively to be the best version of myself. You encouraged me when times were rough. Congratulations to each of you individually and collectively, I'm impressed with your careers and the example you have set for others. Way to go, Poplar Bluff!

Most importantly, I would like to thank God for the gifts that you've given me, for the seeds of which you planted in me for your vision you continue to nurture in me.

I would like to thank my brothers in Christ: Brother Guy Branch, Pastor Byron Jones, Brother Henry Cooper, Brother Rodney Chasson, and Brother LaVert Hamel. It's been great connecting with you each morning. Praying, lifting each other up, sharing our common interests and praying for one another: Iron Sharpens Iron. Thank you for your kindness, the challenging conversations and wisdom. Thank you for your ability to listen and to share. Being transparent and your willingness to put God first each and every morning in your life; to be men of character, value and integrity. Thank you for setting a positive example for me to follow. Bless you!

INTRODUCTION: 30 PLUS YEARS

During my thirty-plus years of being employed in corporate America, plus a few years of U.S. Army experience, I have had the opportunity to learn from leaders (the good, the bad, and the ugly) and their leadership infrastructure.

I can recall my first day of U.S. Army Basic Training, aka "boot camp," at Fort Leonard Wood in Missouri. Upon arrival on the base, fearful thoughts dictated my mindset. I was afraid of the unknown, taunted by the stories and myths shared by veterans, close family, and friends who had previously served their country. When our bus pulled up to our barracks, my soon-to-be living quarters, we were met by yelling, voices of authoritative command, and criticism. "You're in the army now," said the young man sitting next to me.

As the bus doors opened, we were told by the awaiting drill sergeants to hurry up, grab your gear, and get moving...NOW!

Confused, I thought, *"What am I doing here? Why did I sign up for this verbal and mental abuse? Can I go home? I want to go home– now!"*

Needless to say, going home was no longer an option. I had volunteered to serve my country, and I needed to provide for my family.

You see, my life's circumstances had also created my experience. I had become a father at an early age and, in the quest to be responsible for my "manly activity," I had dropped out of college and gotten married. Joining the Army was one way I could get a jumpstart in life, provide for my family, and serve my country– all at once. Nevertheless, I quickly realized that this was going to be an experience. I would need to settle my thoughts and attempt to embrace the unknown.

While serving, I had ideas, suggestions, and recommendations I thought could help the outcome of our goals and objectives. However, because of my rank of Private, I had little to no say-so, which I found frustrating. While I respect the chain of command, as we all should respect the design to accomplish the purpose of the military, I felt extremely stifled.

As the time approached when I'd be able to separate from the military, people whom I cared about, loved, and respected strongly suggested that I stay in. They recommended that I "play it safe" in order to be able to take care of my family, which was, of course, the right thing to do. These well-meaning folks told me, "At least you have a job, you're getting a steady paycheck, and you have insurance," and "There are no jobs for someone without a college education."

But that's not what I wanted to do. So, I did a self-inventory: I assessed my skills and talents, and how they might connect with my purpose and passion in life. Granted, it was hard to identify exactly what that was, but I knew what I did *not* want, which was to be constantly told what to do and how to do it without having any input.

I decided I would take the reins of my life: to separate from the military and take a chance on myself. I prayed a lot, I asked for guidance, and I sought out people who were doing things that I wanted to do, but wasn't sure how. I was lucky I found mentors early in life, and was able to find folks who took a chance on me. That's what propelled me and helped me transition from active military duty to the civilian sector.

In March of 1987, I had fulfilled all of my military duties and earned my honorary discharge. I then applied for a job at a Mitsubishi dealership as a car salesman in Nashville, Tennessee. To begin with, the job description said, *"No college education required,"* and included a few questions that got my attention: *"Do you love people? Are you a good communicator? Would you like to earn an unlimited income?"*

Yes, I said to myself. All of these qualifications were well within my wheelhouse, and potential unlimited income sounded good.

On my first day of training, there was a group of twelve people who started together. Initially, I thought, *Why are there so many of us at one time? Will I be competing with them?*

The sales manager summoned all of us new hires into the conference room. He welcomed us to the dealership and stated that it was his job to motivate us, encourage us, whip us into mental shape, and prepare us to go out there and *sell, sell, sell!*

What he said next would impact my life forever. His words would teach me what to do and what *not* to do as a sales professional. "I want you to meet, greet, lie, and cheat," he said. "I want you to look them in the eye and tell them what they want to hear. I want you to rip off their heads, shit down their throats, and sell the f***ing car!"

I was in shock. My Midwestern values did not align with this manager's philosophy. I could definitely meet and greet, but the thought of having to *lie* and *cheat* absolutely did not resonate with me.

I noticed the behavioral responses of my new team members. While some looked bewildered, several of them were pumped up and excited about this new opportunity... They had no problem with the idea of manipulating and deceiving their customers.

I struggled with it, because I didn't want to be unemployed, but I ultimately decided not to stay with this car dealership. Because of my lack of college education, I assumed I needed to stay in sales. So I began to identify companies who were looking for the same set of skills I knew I had. I found a plethora of them; companies who were looking to hire based on communication skills, ability to interact with others, and to provide customer service. They did not require a college education, but these jobs also did not pay a salary; they were "commission only," so they were willing to take a chance on you.

I went to work for a wholesale jewelry company, selling to retail businesses. I would encourage them to offer our product in their storefronts as a way for them to earn extra money.

One of the first places I walked into was a tanning salon. Now imagine me, an African American male, walking into a tanning salon in Nashville, Tennessee, and the expression on this young lady's face!

She finally asked, "How can I help you?"

I answered, "I'm here to get a tan."

We both laughed and that broke the ice. They did not purchase my product, unfortunately, but I saw it as "failing forward." After all, sales was a fairly new arena for me. I was getting practice in meeting people "where they are," and building rapport. So, even when I didn't make a sale, I was building relationships and learning that, even in our differences, we can have some engagement, a cordial conversation, and sometimes, a good laugh about those differences!

The Desired Outcome Is Positive

"If you want to change your life, change your mind."

It's as simple and as complicated as that. We can literally change our experience if we change our *perspective*. A great deal of research has been done by neuroscientists that verify this to be not just a "woo-woo" concept, but a verifiable scientific fact. And we already understand it: *Is the glass half empty, or is it half full?* We know the answer just depends on your perspective. But we don't always apply this knowledge effectively in our own lives. I'm going to share a personal story about how I learned the power of changing one's mind.

I didn't know my father until late in my adolescence. I had yearned to identify who he was and what he was all about. I heard rumors that he had been a great athlete, he was a teacher, and he was all the things I wanted my dad to be.

When I finally met him, we developed a great rapport and relationship, and I was glad to be his son— but that didn't happen overnight. My dad had his own characteristics, his own behaviors, and some of them did not align with my expectations of what a father should be. I could easily justify blaming, being critical and judgmental, but that wasn't working well for me. It created emotions that were the opposite of what I wanted to feel. I didn't want to feel sad, I didn't want to feel displaced, and I didn't want to feel like an outcast from his life any longer.

I made up my mind that I wanted to enjoy my life— I could do something about this situation. Sure, I couldn't change my father, but I could change how I perceived him and interacted with him. If I was ever going to have a chance at building a good relationship with my dad, I would need to learn how to love him unconditionally; meaning, I'd have to accept him for who he was.

By focusing on my goal of a positive outcome, and practicing loving unconditionally as a way to rise above my painful thoughts and feelings, I started to see people and situations differently. I could more easily accept people for who they were, and that began to open new opportunities in less-than-perfect relationships, not just with my father, but with others as well. My desired outcome was positive which went hand in hand with a new belief that great things could happen with my dad. And they did.

Expect Great Things to Happen

Life can be difficult; it can be miserable. Yet, if that's *all* I'm extracting from an experience, a positive outcome seems impossible. In reality, it doesn't have to be as bad as it appears; good things are also happening, even if we don't recognize them, *yet*.

Just like everyone else, I get upset, I get frustrated, I get pissed off. But, for me, it's temporary. Life is happening to me just as it is to everyone else, and I have a right to complain and moan just like everyone else. And while I do allow myself to feel the emotions, I do *not* allow myself to rest there, because that becomes a pattern of an emotional experience I don't care to rest in. We're all entitled to a bad moment, but I refuse to stay in a negative mindset. I have to remain positive and optimistic, simply because I don't like feeling depressed – I want to do something about it. Even when life is at its worst, I remember that someone else has it worse than me. And there are too many alternatives and options that become available when we focus on creating a positive outcome.

I want you to feel your emotions and whatever is connected to the experience of a moment; try not to focus solely on the "doom and gloom."

Instead, ask yourself, *Why is this happening? What can I potentially do about it? How could I expand my point of view?*

Consider the possibility that whatever is unfolding, as unpleasant as it may seem, it's happening <u>for you</u> rather than <u>to you</u>. When we believe something's happening <u>to us</u>, we get stuck in a funk; but if we ask ourselves, *why is this happening for me?*, it literally expands our whole mindset.

Now we can consider, *Are there any benefits to this? Is this a growth moment that's preparing me for something greater in my future?* Or, for example, when things aren't moving forward, it might be, *Hey, maybe this is a place where I need to rest right now*. You can choose how you're going to experience each moment. When your goal and intention is a positive outcome, your experience is going to shift.

So when someone tells me they're having a "bad" day, I'm asking, "What happened all those other hours in the day when you could have potentially changed that?"

It does take practice to think differently about your current situation. I encourage you, right now, to make up your mind that you desire positive outcomes. When you do that, you can expect great things to happen.

Components of Success

While conducting the research to start my own company – RDM Management Group – I studied both successful athletes and successful business professionals. I sought to understand their similarities and where they overlapped.

What they all had in common was Self-Confidence, Self-Discipline, Emotional Intelligence and Motivation. In this book, we're going to explore these tools and their guiding principles, along with something I see as a foundation for all of them: Self-Awareness.

Once you learn the tools in this book they become transferable skills, you'll be able to apply them in any area of your life, not just business. I encourage you to embrace them.

Keep in mind, I sincerely desire a positive outcome for myself and everyone I meet – *including you.* So, let's begin, and expect great things to happen!

SECTION 1:
SELF-AWARENESS

CHAPTER 1:
THE INTROSPECTIVE VIEW

What I call "The Introspective View" is defined by self-examination: Figuring out your own motivation and your own purpose. One of the things I learned early on is that, as I approach the complexities of life, I need to do a self-assessment.

This is what I call giving myself a "check-up from the neck up." I mean, that is where the problems usually are: in my head!

If a situation seems counter to your desired outcome, it may be an area of opportunity to increase your self-awareness.

In his book *Emotional Intelligence*, author Travis Bradberry's first component of emotional intelligence is awareness of yourself, or *self-awareness*. That is, the ability to recognize and understand your own moods and emotions, as well as their effect on others.

Remember, the desired outcome is positive. So, if I'm feeling stressed, if I've been caught up in the complexities of the day, before I interact with my staff members or any other spheres of influence, what might I do to achieve a positive outcome?

I could first go for a walk, I could take a coffee break, I could meditate, I could incorporate a training in mindfulness. There are multiple things I could do, but first I would need to be consciously aware of myself and my mood in order to recognize I'm not at my best right now.

Whether you're aware of it or not, chances are that the impact of not being the best version of yourself is going to be negative. And that negative impact is multiplied when interacting with team members.

As a leader, you're setting the stage for people to follow, you're leading by example, and because of that, you need to be consciously aware of the example you're setting for others.

When things are easy, when life is fun and exciting, when I'm accomplishing goals and objectives, I find it's easy to practice self-awareness. But when I'm under stress, when I'm challenged, when I have to meet deadlines and the pressure is building, that is the real test.

At times, I was looking for other people to validate me or direct me. Validation and guidance are important, depending on what you're working on. There is also a need, however, to do an internal inventory, and to make sure that your motivation is in line with what you're trying to accomplish. It pays to evaluate your mental space around your desired outcome.

I've found that sometimes my motivations were manipulative, sometimes my motivations weren't necessarily holistic, or weren't in line with a positive outcome for others as well as myself. Being selfish is a human component that we all must face in an honest self-evaluation. It's not always fun or easy, but taking the *introspective view* is illuminating and provides opportunities to grow.

There's a book a client asked me to read called Principles. In this book, the author, Ray Dalio, explains that human beings suffer most from two things: one is **ego** and the other is **blind spots.**

Ego

Ego is something we all have and it's quite often unregulated. In the simplest sense, it is how we perceive ourselves.

I'm a confident person, I want to feel good about myself, and I encourage others to do so, but there is a very delicate balance between confidence and cockiness. I try to regulate that to find the right amount of confidence, where it doesn't offend someone or discount other people. I want to be very careful about that.

A healthy amount of ego and confidence is important. Self-esteem makes you feel good about yourself, but it's too much if you're discounting others, discarding others, or manipulating others.

That's when you want to do a self-assessment. Taking an introspective view can put it in balance, and you may want to apologize if you offended someone based on your ego.

As a leader, a healthy amount of ego is important. You're being paid to get things done, you're getting paid to motivate and lead others. But if you're not careful, too much of that can make other people feel discounted and unappreciated, and they won't do as good of a job for you.

Self-awareness will help you assess your ego and how it can "act out" at times, meaning your cocky behavior is not helping you with your desired outcomes. Self-regulation will allow you to make adjustments.

On the other side of the ego coin, some folks are more reserved which may be a sort of submissive personality where people position themselves to be unintentionally discounted by others. They tend to avoid confrontation. Even when it's necessary to stand up for themselves, they don't want to deal with it, because of how it makes them feel. They may be even more concerned with how it makes others feel. So it becomes a tendency and a habit of discounting one's self, leaving one's own needs and goals out of the equation, which leads to being taken for granted and disrespected by others. If you have this tendency, you may need to build up your ego.

A work friend of mine would call her husband a "doormat" because people walk all over him and that frustrated the heck out of her. She wanted him to speak up for himself. Of course, this is very subjective based on their spousal relationship, but I've had the opportunity to interact with people who do behave like a doormat. They often go above and beyond for others, but their efforts go unacknowledged.

By frequently saying things like, "you decide," and "everything is okay," when it's really not, these individuals discount themselves and their own value, which unfortunately, leaves them feeling frustrated.

So, if you identify at all with the "doormat" title, it's time for a self-assessment and learning these *Core Principles of High-*

ly Effective Business Professionals, so you can generate more positive outcomes, and start getting more of what you want out of life.

Blind Spots

Blind spots are what we're missing and failing to take into account. Just like driving a car, we may see a lot, but we can't see everything around us at once. A blind spot is being unaware of something about yourself or your behavior, or the impact you're having on other people.

No one knows you better than you know yourself, but, if you're human, you have blind spots. None of us can automatically understand the impact of our lack of self-awareness and how our moods and actions are impacting other people. Often, we believe we're self-aware and know exactly what we're doing, **yet we do not know what we do not know**. Those are the *blind* spots.

As you navigate through the complexities of life, you need to be able to understand and recognize the emotions in yourself as well as others. This requires patience and listening, which are skill sets that can be practiced. In order to communicate effectively and strategically, you need both self-awareness and awareness of others to help you manage your own behavior and your relationships.

Now that we've identified what ego and blind spots are, I'm going to discuss some of the most damaging blind spots for both ourselves and others: unconscious biases.

CHAPTER 2:
UNCONSCIOUS BIAS

As we are about to explore unconscious bias, I'd like for you to first contemplate three questions:

1) What does unconscious bias mean to you?
2) What do you know about unconscious bias?
3) Is unconscious bias important to you? If yes, why? If not, why not?

One might hear or read the term "unconscious bias" and assume we're talking about race, but it's about much more than that. Race is a factor, but only one part of the equation.

Bias is a tendency, trend, inclination, feeling, or opinion, especially one that is preconceived and not necessarily based on reason or facts.

Bias often refers to a prejudice or unreasonably hostile feelings or opinions about a particular social group or demographic; for example, the idea that "lawyers always lie."

Bias can be positive, such as assuming if someone is slim it means they're physically healthy, or that someone who wears glasses is smart.

Our minds tend to make many decisions and judgements about other people very quickly, very reactively, almost automatically, and we may be totally unaware of the influence of our own bias. That's *unconscious bias* – when we're not consciously aware that we're making these snap judgments off of our own bias rather than through reason and fact.

You know the old adage, *Don't judge a book by its cover?*

We're all taught this bit of wisdom from a young age, yet we instinctively and automatically judge books by their covers *all* the time. We see and judge each other through the lens of our own biases, and it happens in an instant.

We often take our own snap judgments as objective facts, but our perspectives are very subjective. Shaped by stories we're told or those we've told ourselves about certain groups, about certain "types" of individuals, we're largely unaware that our unconscious lens gets in the way of seeing people and situations as they actually are.

If the research is correct, it says that every single one of us has unconscious biases. We have unconscious biases about the country or city in which a person was born, their religious beliefs, socio-economic status, parental status, race, ethnicity, sexual preference, clothing style, and pretty much anything else you can think of.

Unconscious bias can prevent us from making objective, sound decisions.

It can cause us to overlook great ideas, undermine others' potential, and create a *less than* ideal work experience for colleagues.

It can interfere with our influential relationships and inter-actions in social gatherings.

By understanding and working to overcome unconscious bias at critical moments, individuals can make better decisions, encourage diverse perspectives and contributions, and provide a more harmonious workplace for all.

Unconscious biases are ingrained in the corporate environment. They're ingrained in our communities. To me, this is a great area of opportunity. When we address our unconscious biases, we can expect great things to happen.

As we dive deeper into an understanding of unconscious bias, let's focus on the introspective view and perspective of this very important topic.

Again, unconscious biases are often stereotypes about certain groups of people, biases that individuals form outside of their own conscious awareness.

Everyone, including the author of this book, holds unconscious beliefs about various social and identity groups. These biases stem from our mind's tendency to organize social worlds by categorizing them.

As we assess these categories, we must ask ourselves the following questions:

What have you heard about this group before?

How has what you heard from someone else shaped or influenced your perspective on the group?

Let's start with communication styles.

There are a variety of communication styles: aggressive, passive-aggressive, submissive, manipulative, and assertive.

It's possible that if someone doesn't communicate in the way that I do, and this happens often in the workplace, especially as a leader, I may judge that book, or those people, by their cover.

And there's not just style, but also pace, pitch, accent, regional expressions, etc. I live in Southern California and when I interact with native Californians it's not unusual for them to ask me where I'm from.

I laugh slightly and ask, "Where do you think I'm from?"

The response typically suggests I'm from the South.

I say, "No, I'm not from the South. I'm from the Midwest – Missouri."

They assume correctly that I'm not a native Californian, because my accent is a little different, but it's not Southern, so there is some kind of unconscious bias making them assume I must be from the South.

How about marriage? Single people often wish they were married, while married people often wish they were single. There are preconceived notions on both sides - the grass would definitely be greener if I could just get married (or divorced!).

How about the military? I am prior military and many of my friends and colleagues are too. When I speak to civilians, they often assume that all military people have PTSD (post-traumatic stress disorder.) Interestingly, according to the research, there are more people in the general population who suffer from PTSD symptoms than do military and former military people.

How about location? When I first moved to the city of Escondido, many people I knew had preconceived notions about Escondido without ever having been there, because of what they had heard. Granted, there are issues and challenges in all cities around this great country of ours, but automatically accepting someone's second- or third-hand idea about a city without having been there oneself is unconscious bias at work.

How about education? As a young man, I was told that without a college degree you could never be successful. That was the unconscious bias that everyone around me had. Well, I only have a high school education, but I have tons of experiential education, which is about what you choose to learn, and I have applied it to build a profitable, well-respected company. Some of the greatest leaders and business successes of our time don't have college degrees either, and I personally know people with master's degrees and PhDs who are out of work and struggling financially.

What about age? I'm a baby boomer and if I hear one more baby boomer disrespectfully complain about a millennial, I think I'm going to lose it. Their unconscious biases about millennials are simply not correct, at least not in my experience. How about getting to know the person for who they actually are before passing judgment on them?

Speaking of pre-judging, *how about race?* Walking around with unconscious preconceived ideas about enormous groups of people based only on the color of their skin is an area of opportunity to get curious and learn.

A friend of mine asked me, "Richard, what can we do as an organization to create a better narrative? What actions and initiatives can we take to improve race relations?"

He also said, "When I see a person of African-American descent, particularly male, with a hoodie on and pants hanging below his waist, I'm instinctively concerned."

This friend told me he was in his neighborhood in Carlsbad and saw a person of color in a hoodie in baggy pants. His first thought was, *Why is this guy in my affluent beach neighborhood? And his next thought was, Should I move to the other side of the street?*

He chose not to cross the street. They exchanged a brief pleasantry as they walked past each other. My friend turned back and saw the guy walk up to his neighbor's house.

When he saw the neighbor later in the day he asked, "Hey, I noticed a person of color walking up to your house this morning, is everything okay?"

The neighbor said, "Of course, everything's okay. The guy you're talking about is my boss; he was coming over for breakfast."

So, my friend was forced to recognize his unconscious bias. He blamed it on the media shaping a narrative, but very often we're judging a book by its cover, like an individual's clothing. By the way, I've often worn a hoodie, particularly in Southern California where it's a common style. There's no reason for anyone to think anything of it, except for the fact that unconscious bias based on appearance quite often dictates our perspective.

What about the workplace? To begin with, research suggests that the average resume is only viewed for about 10 to 15 seconds. How can anyone evaluate a potential candidate that quickly? I would venture that there are at least occasional unconscious biases triggered by any number of things, such as the name of the individual, their gender, or even their address.

Often employers have unconsciously biased expectations of their employees based on their marital status – assuming a single person is automatically more flexible and available for extra work hours than a married person, especially those who have children. It often doesn't occur to them that the single employee may be in a serious relationship too, may also be going to school, or caring for a sick relative.

One of my clients out East explained to me that she prefers hiring people with military experience. She works for the Department of Defense on a military base, but the jobs she's hiring for are open to civilians. Still, she has a preference for folks with military experience because she believes they are better able to serve military clients and are more disciplined workers. The interesting part is there are many civilians working in support of the military who can be equally, if not *more*, qualified than their military counterparts, especially when the job qualifications are not exclusive to the military, such as bookkeeping, maintaining websites, etc.

A difference in thinking styles can trigger unconscious bias at work. There's strategic thinking and logical thinking; lots of different styles and having a variety to work on issues and challenges in the workplace can be very beneficial.

So if you're only hiring people with one type of thinking style, you can create what we call "groupthink" which is everyone always in agreement, when in reality, the best way to obtain a solution to a problem is often by coming at it from different perspectives and ways of thinking.

One of my clients with a company wrote a job description that included a college degree was required but they weren't getting enough applicants, so they reluctantly opened it up to more diverse people with different educational levels. Finally, they realized that a college degree wasn't required or even necessary for the role, more important was *previous experience*. They had made a college degree the main requirement without thinking it through. *Unconscious bias.*

Age in the workplace? The fact of the matter is, there could be up to five different generations within the workforce today. How we view these different age groups and what these individuals have to contribute is really important.

Confirmation Bias

Unconscious biases can be reinforced by *confirmation bias.*

Confirmation bias happens when you often get validation on your beliefs and biases from your own social group, your family, your co-workers, etc. Like-minded individuals may validate and confirm what you think about a certain group, and if you don't make your own observations and have conversations with members of the group in question to get to know them first-hand, people in your own circle may confirm that your judgements are correct, even though they may very well be incorrect. This gives rise to the groupthink I just mentioned – when a group of people agree with each other unquestioningly, and may even stifle alternative points of view.

CHAPTER 3:
CURIOSITY IS A STRENGTH

Curiosity applies to the introspective view and increasing your own self-awareness, as well as being curious about how to become the best leader you can possibly be.

When it comes to other people, curiosity can transform confusion and frustration into clarity and understanding, helping you to overcome your blind spots and unconscious biases.

If we don't understand someone or we are frustrated by them, say someone falls into one of our unconscious bias categories, if we don't ask the individual or members of that group for clarification, we're going to make up our own answers.

If I get "insight" from my own peer group, it may be based on the same bias I'm carrying around, which is "confirmation bias."

What I encourage folks to do is to get curious and ask questions. For example, if you wonder why someone is wearing baggy pants, as in the earlier example, why don't you go and ask them?

This is one of the ways to get to know a person as an individual, as opposed to stereotyping them based on the influence of your own unconscious bias. This is what I mean by getting curious. Don't assume and avoid groupthink— just ask that particular person.

And if you're the person being asked this kind of question, which may seem silly or insulting to you at first glance, ask yourself if it's coming from a good place of healthy curiosity. If someone wants to learn about you, it's important not to make them feel awkward or bad about it.

I encourage curiosity as a way to overcome unconscious bias, so it's important for me not to get offended if someone asks me why I'm wearing a hoodie. By listening to others holistically and objectively to the best of my ability, fully present rather than formulating a response while they're talking, I have a much better chance of understanding their perspective and giving them a meaningful answer. It's a very delicate balance and very subjective, depending on what I'm being asked, and how.

I especially encourage leaders to be curious. Go ahead and ask the particular person you're curious about, and do it in a very thoughtful way. This means you first have to identify your own level of self-awareness; that's going to be really important and make all the difference in this kind of conversation.

The ability to ask someone an uncomfortable question without offending them is a social skill involving emotional intelligence that I will discuss in detail in section five of this book.

Self-Awareness Leads to Self-Confidence

Doing your introspective view work and increasing self-awareness is not just to root out blind spots and areas that could use some improvement. A big part of becoming more aware of yourself is identifying your own abilities and talents and positive character traits. Knowing your unique gifts makes it possible to know all of you and to be your authentic self.

If you want to lead others effectively, it is very important to become comfortable in your own skin. As a matter of fact, it allows you to show up as the truest, most confident, best version of yourself.

Being your authentic self comes with responsibility; me being authentic doesn't mean I have the right to offend you. I need to have a level of self-awareness on how I come across at *the same time* that I'm being confident in who I am.

When you can be true to yourself while also taking into account how your mood and actions are impacting other people, that is a skillset you can practice, and it builds self-confidence. You can be authentic, knowing the best version of you is on display and interacting with everyone else in a positive, constructive way.

SECTION 2:
SELF-CONFIDENCE

CHAPTER 4:
SELF-CONFIDENCE

Simply put, self-confidence is trust and belief in your own capabilities, judgments, and in your own ability to successfully handle day-to-day challenges. Self-confidence is a personal attribute that you can cultivate. It's also the basis for a lot of interpersonal skills.

During my corporate career, there were often times when I did not have the hard skills to accomplish the task at hand. The one thing that propelled me throughout my business career was the ability to interact and get along well with others. My innate interpersonal skills are what allowed me to maintain and increase my self-confidence.

Athletes must have self-confidence. To even put one's self in an environment in which the sole purpose is to compete with others, it's imperative to believe in one's own power and ability, and for that belief to influence others' to also believe in one's skills, talents, and ability to deliver them consistently.

Self-confidence is equally important for business professionals. If you're going to be successful as an individual contributor or leader, you must believe in yourself. Knowing and trusting in your own skills, talents, and abilities is equally as important as it is for an athlete. And in business, competition with others often plays a part. Whether you're competing on the sports field or in the business landscape, confidence in yourself and your abilities is paramount.

The Importance of Confidence

A favorite pastime for many Americans is watching football. It's an exciting game of brute force, strategy, and execution. One team is playing the offense, the other, the defense. One of the primary goals of the defense is to prevent the offense from scoring. The defense will study the other team's offense and design plays to prevent them from gaining yards on the field toward the goal posts.

An aggressive defense will disrupt the offense through tackles – physical hard-hitting assaults on their opponents. One of their many tactics is to cause the offense to fumble the ball or intercept it, which is when the quarterback throws the ball to their own team but the defense intercepts the throw, gets control of the ball, and runs for a touchdown.

If this defensive strategy has ever worked against your favorite team, the initial impact can be devastating. Your reaction might be frustration or disbelief. Analytical reasoning will take over your mind as you ask yourself, *what the heck was the offense thinking?* If only the offense would have listened to you, they would have seen this coming and avoided this series of unwanted events! Depending on how invested you are in the outcome of the game, your stress and anxiety levels may begin to peak.

Similarly, as we pursue our own goals and objectives, we face difficulties in life that can impact our level of confidence – the things we may be going through, the challenging moments.

We also face the opposition of self-doubt, uncertainty, and fear intruding upon our minds. This internal opposition can undermine our self-confidence as it pertains to our ability to accomplish a particular task or goal. The emotional impact of these feelings is equally harmful as we enter the arena of self-improvement. If we're unable to outwit these negative internal attacks, our aspirations for a positive future will be delayed, or even missed.

So if my goal is to be a motivational speaker and the first time I stand up to speak I see anyone talking, laughing, not paying attention, or falling asleep, that could erode my level of self-confidence. It's like an attack from the opposition that, if I allow it to marinate in my head, would distract me, leading me to believe no one is paying attention at all. Now, to my mind, everyone is talking, or everyone is falling asleep! I can't stay focused on my task at hand and my larger goal.

The reality is, as we begin to achieve our goals, there are going to be distractions and setbacks, we will fumble the ball at times, or even have complete failures. It was motivational speaker Les Brown who said something that has really helped me deal with the failures: *"Anything worth doing is worth doing badly, until you get it right."*

Lack of Self-Confidence

There have been many times, up to this day, when I've had reasonable self-doubts and lagging self-confidence. As I flash back to those experiences, I've concluded my self-confidence has been formed by my previous personal experiences and my mindset, which itself has been shaped by what individual people and society as a whole have told me, and through comparing my own outcomes with the successes of others.

An example of how my mindset has impacted my self-confidence is demonstrated as I write this book. The thought of writing a book first entered my mind several years ago. I believed my work, my life experiences, and my corporate background could help others achieve their goals and objectives in life.

As I contemplated writing a book, my initial thoughts brought me joy and excitement. I thought about all the lives my book could positively impact. Readers would be able to take the concepts I learned through my life's journey, put them into practice in their day-to-day activities, and yield the results they seek. The book would inspire others to accept gold nuggets into their thought processes and deploy them as needed. I aspired to be my readers' inspiration and provide them with valuable tools for their success.

But, then, my thoughts began to shift away from writing a book. I asked myself, *Richard, do you really think people would read your book? Why would they read it? You've never written a book before. Is this just another one of your sound-good ideas that feels right for the moment, just to allow you to think optimistically about yourself and your future?*

Furthermore, I've personally struggled with reading in the past. My ability to remain focused while reading an author's words needed some improvement. My mind would often wander to thoughts unrelated to the words in front of me. I asked myself, *would readers do the same with my book?* Anxiety and doubt began to answer my questions in an alarming, pictorial way. I visualized zero book sales, critical comments, and embarrassment in front of my peers.

To break through that, I began to consciously shift my thoughts from a worst-case scenario to expecting great things to happen.

A few years ago, I had the opportunity to facilitate a veteran's transition training called Reboot. The Reboot Training is designed to help active-duty service members transition into civilian life. At that time, I was introduced to the teachings of business educator Lou Tice, who wasn't the first to share this concept: **"If you want to change your life, change your mind."**

These words of wisdom helped me shift my perspective on myself, and to return to imagining the positive outcome this book could have in the lives of its readers.

Know Your Value

First of all, value is very subjective. It varies from person to person, and that's why it's important for you to be fully aware of your own value. Otherwise, you're constantly trying to get validation from someone else and you'll end up serving someone else without serving your own goals. Granted, we do get some of this confirmation from our peer group, a parent, a sibling or a friend, and that's great. By the way, you do want to surround yourself with positive people who care about you and appreciate you. They can help you identify and align with your own value.

However, if you never internally identify who you are and your own worth, there will always be an empty space within you– until you understand your own value.

How do I do that?, you may wonder. A good place to start is by asking yourself, *What do I enjoy? What are my natural interests and talents?* Your answers may even be contradictory to what someone else thinks or believes, and that's okay. You want to cultivate your own self-awareness and self-validation. Knowing that you have something of worth and value to bring to the table is very important.

I preface this by saying your self-validation and sense of self-worth needs to be healthy. You want to communicate your value with confidence without coming across as self-aggrandizing or cocky. Having great talents and abilities doesn't give one the right to disregard the talents and abilities of others.

I can recall when I decided to publish my online sales training course: thoughts of teaching students via the Internet was a novel idea to me. The favorable feedback from my face-to-face facilitation and various trainings encouraged me to embark on this task.

Initially, I was unsure how I was going to do it. I began to pray for direction, clarity, and favor. I consulted my wife, Eleasa, my mom, Reeda, professional colleagues, and friends in my inner circle. Every single person supported me.

Of course, with any new goal comes new challenges.

Challenge #1: I had no idea where I would house my content. Would you believe that the very next morning I received a call from an online training company looking to expand their education and training portfolio from universities and colleges by partnering with training consultants and business coaches like myself and others?

Challenge #2: I did not have the financial resources to professionally record and edit each video training module.

The next day, I had a networking lunch with my friend, Janet Bark. We were both looking forward to catching each other up on our latest and greatest triumphs and challenges. I shared with Janet my quest to take my classroom virtual. She was really excited for me. Janet asked, "Who is going to record your training video sessions?"

I shamelessly told her I was going to use my phone.

Janet looked at me and said, "No, you are not!"

"I don't have much of a choice," I said. "I'm committed to getting this done, and getting it done now."

Janet shared with me her concerns over attempting this task on a mobile device. What she said next shocked me. "Richard, I'll record the sessions for you. For free."

You see, Janet is a professional photographer and was interested in increasing her brand and her reach as a videographer. The universe was in alignment with my goal!

And, yet, for a period of time, I still did not move forward. Why not? It was my lack of confidence in my own value, compounded by F.E.A.R.

CHAPTER 5:
FEAR AND F.E.A.R.

What is this thing called fear?

In my lifetime, I've uncovered two types of fear.

The first is healthy. It's the type of fear designed to keep you and I safe, to keep us out of harm's way. To keep us on the straight and narrow. To keep us focused on accomplishing our goals and objectives.

The second one is F.E.A.R. This stands for "False Evidence Appearing Real."

False meaning it's a fallacy, not a fact.

Evidence Appearing Real is what we've seen or been told that we take to be an irrefutable indication of the future, such as memories of past mistakes and failures leading to thoughts like, *I will never be able to succeed.* It could be something like, *No one in our family has ever been able to...* or, *If you stay home and don't try, you won't get hurt.*

F.E.A.R. (False Evidence Appearing Real) is just that. Imaginary scenarios, depictions of situations that may look and even feel quite realistic, often run over and over in our minds until they convince us that the worst-case scenario is going to happen.

This is F.E.A.R. in action. This is the mind trying to protect us from unwanted outcomes. The problem is, by provoking all of our worst fears, it stops us from taking the risks we need to take in order to pursue our own greatness. It makes us say 'no' to the very opportunities that could bring the most benefits and rewards.

When I entered the wireless industry as a business sales professional in 1997, I was one of only two people in the company who did not have a cellular or a wireless background. Many of the other new sales reps came from competing companies.

Days after our onboarding, the district managers asked everyone to put together a list of prospects and previous clients they had acquired prior to joining Nextel. These prospects would be exclusive to the person who suggested them for sixty days. If progress had not been made, the prospects were open to other team members to call upon. My family and I had just relocated to Houston a couple of months prior from living in Oahu, Hawaii, and my wife Eleasa had just given birth to our youngest daughter, Evana. The only businessperson I had formed a relationship with was my wonderful sister-in-law, Susie. Susie worked for a major hospital. Based on my limited exposure to businesses in Houston, I placed her name on my list, just to save face. Meanwhile, many of my cohorts compiled legal pages full of business names, contacts, and phone numbers. I had only one! My lack of resources created both fear and F.E.A.R. I was perhaps rightfully concerned about my lack of contacts and assumed my team members' chances of success were far greater than my own.

This fear forced me to become focused and disciplined in my day-to-day sales activity. I read and reviewed the corporate training manual, also known as our *Sales Playbook*. This manual gave me the blueprint on how to successfully sell the Nextel products and services. The manual instructed me to make fifty cold calls from the yellow pages and knock on twenty doors to various businesses *per day*. This activity was supposed to generate two appointments/presentations per day, or ten per week. We were expected to close 50% of our appointments. Each sale, on average, was three units. Three units multiplied by five successful appointments equals fifteen sales per week. Fifteen sales per week, multiplied by four weeks, equated to my proscribed sales goal of sixty units per month, with an average revenue of $45 per sale.

On the same day I first studied the manual, the managers called a team meeting after lunch to discuss our sales plan. The compensation model was exciting; the only thing I had to do was meet or exceed my sales quota. One of the managers also introduced a plan called P.I.P. which was the Performance Improvement Plan. This was a plan I did not want to be a part of because if any salesperson missed their sales quota for three consecutive months, he or she would be placed on a P.I.P. If, by chance, you missed your P.I.P. objectives, you would no longer be employed with the company. This compounded my fears, along with the added pressure of needing to save up enough money to move my family out of my mother-in-law's house– it was all starting to wear on me.

However, this was a *healthy* fear because I did not allow it to paralyze me. Rather, it motivated me to remain focused and disciplined. Not only did I exceed my sales goals, I won several awards, prizes, and a promotion. Plus, I was able to move my family out of my mother-in-law's house.

Other common fears include the fear of failure and the fear of the unknown. I know that for me to achieve my life's purpose, I will have to do and go through some things that I have never experienced before.

Impostor Syndrome

Self-confidence is a belief in oneself, one's skills, talents, abilities and acumen. However, it is never constant; it's subject to be quite volatile.

Yes, I feel good about what I know today, but if I'm placed into an environment or take on a new task or goal that I'm unfamiliar with, my self-confidence becomes, let's say, subdued.

I hear from leaders all the time, people who are looking to grow within their careers. They say, "I want to move up and take on a new job."

They have an interview that convinces their leaders they're the right person to take on the job, helping to take their organization to a new level of success. But when they run into an area they haven't experienced before, which is only natural since they just started a new job, doubts arise in their minds: *Am I the right person for this role? Can I even do this job?*

Until they have experienced components of success in the new position, no matter how big or small, they think they may not be the right person for the job after all, and they don't have the level of confidence required to say to their supervisor, "You know what, I don't know how to do this such-and-so."

They lack the self-confidence to realize, *If my leaders promote me into this position, they will support me as I grow into it.*

Instead, they think, *If I expose myself to this leader that there are things I don't know, they might think that they promoted the wrong person.*

That's *Impostor Syndrome* setting in. So, they suffer in silence.

We need to recognize that once we take on a new task or a new goal, where we haven't done certain things before, we're not going to have the same level of confidence– even if we initially felt confident envisioning being that role.

Whenever we take on something foreign, something we haven't experienced before, self-doubts arise that can lead to the F.E.A.R. We may even seek out false evidence to convince ourselves, *I can't do this because I haven't done it before.*

If you have a conversation with a family member, friend, or someone of influence, and they say, "That seems daunting" or, "That sounds pretty scary," or even, "I don't know if you should do that," it's like getting outside validation to make our false evidence appear even more real. We've all been there.

As I shared earlier, even with this book, I started off thinking, *Yes I can do this*, but then I started to have doubts. When I shared ideas for the book and other people didn't give me the validation I was looking for, I talked myself out of it for a while. *It's not a good idea, I told myself. I'm not a writer, who's gonna read this anyway?*

Consider this: whatever obstacles you're facing today, chances are you have overcome equally big challenges in the past, which prepared you for your future. This may very well be difficult and daunting today, but taking an introspective view can help. Looking internally, you will recognize that you've already accomplished difficult things your entire life, and you've already had plenty of successes. This just so happens to be a new challenge. Fear is still going to come up, but you can discipline yourself to rise to any challenge.

Yes, you will have moments of failure which may shake your self-confidence. We all know what that feels like, too.

However, I've learned to trust my inspiration and experiences. No one can take my experiences away from me. I look at two successful men like Tony Robbins and Les Brown, and I see that their expertise is based on their individual experiences. They're simply sharing their experiences and imparting lessons learned, and it's helped so many people that they're household names now.

I have my experiences, you have your experiences, and who is to tell us those experiences are incorrect or failures? They were preparing us for our next steps in life.

Stop Being "Your Own Worst Critic"

I was hanging out with my mom a few years ago and sharing with her about my new business and how it wasn't quite where I wanted it to be. I began to speak negatively about my disappointment around the level I was at.

"Richard," she said, "you know we are our own worst critics."

Right then and there, it hit me like a ton of bricks. We've been told that since we were maybe two years old, that we are our own worst critics. I said, "Mom, you know what, I do not have to be my own worst critic."

I didn't realize there was a choice *until that moment*. I don't have to be my own worst critic!

I made a decision. From that moment on, I was no longer going to impart self-inflicted wounds upon myself, knocking myself down. I had a new goal now: to become my own biggest fan, my biggest cheerleader. Yes, there are areas in which I need to improve and need to grow, but I don't have to beat myself up. Instead, I can encourage myself, and I can expect great things to happen.

"Allow Yourself To Absorb The Emotional Impact Of Your Fear, While Pushing Forward"

I encourage you not to rest in fear because it can paralyze you and prevent you from taking a chance. When you do step into a bigger position, you're in the process of expanding your experience, so how could you possibly be as confident as you were? As you move up the ladder, you will be called upon to

49

do things you haven't done before. It's only natural to have to grow in order to fit into your new role. So trust in yourself and go for it.

Dealing With the Negative Voices in Our Heads

Self-talk is a conversation you have with yourself, about yourself.

No one can hear these conversations except you. Self-talk is an internal self-assessment. It tells you how you see yourself.

I've discovered that, as I embark upon a new goal, I am also subject to doubts about achieving that goal. If I'm not careful with my thought patterns, I will procrastinate on putting in any effort and/or abandon the goal altogether, even if it's for my betterment, or it is a great opportunity for my business.

Over the years, I've asked my audience of adult learners to rate their self-talk using a color system. Like a traffic light, I use the colors red, yellow, and green.

Red: Most of the conversations you have with yourself and about yourself are *negative*.

Yellow: Your internal conversations are a 50/50 hybrid, meaning half of the conversations you have with yourself, about yourself are equally positive and negative in nature.

Green: Indicates the majority of conversations you're having with yourself, about yourself are *positive*.

Rate Your Self-Talk

Through my own research and polling my audiences, I've found that, on average, over 70% of people are "in the red" where most of their self-talk is a *negative* assessment of them-selves. Over 75% of people polled claim to be in the **red** or **yel-low** category.

This leads me to conclude that it's more common than not for negative thoughts about one's self to dominate self-talk and, as a result, most of us see ourselves in a *negative* light.

Replace Negative Self-Talk with Positive Affirmations

Louise Hay, American motivational author, dedicated her life to teaching people how to live a positive and empowered life, often with the aid of positive statements and beliefs, which she called *affirmations*. Louise taught that your point of power is always in the present moment, where you plant the mental seeds for creating new experiences.

Positive affirmations are statements that affirm something to be true. They can be applied to present-day yourself, or in your future.

One of the primary uses of positive affirmations is to replace negative thinking with positive thoughts. The more we actively change the internal conversations with ourselves from negative to positive, **the more inclined we become to remove the emotional barriers that prevent us from being the best version ourselves.**

Positive affirmations are the opposite of negative thinking. For example, instead of telling myself *I'm not an author,* or *no one wants to read my book*, I can replace those negative thoughts by saying:

I am a talented and successful author.

My book is in demand.

People are encouraged and excited when they read my book.

If You Think You Can, You Can

If you want to know what your future looks like, listen to the conversations you're having with yourself today. Auto industry pioneer Henry Ford famously stated, ***"Whether you think you can, or you think you can't—you're right."***

To be honest, when I first heard this quote, it pissed me off.

I was young and I was upset that my few sales jobs hadn't worked out. I was becoming really frustrated with myself because I wasn't accomplishing the goals or achieving the sort of heights I was seeking.

But if it really was all up to me and my mindset, I could no longer blame my circumstances on people, places, or things. If I wanted to change my current situation, I first would have to change my way of thinking. That's what I resisted at first.

Once I finally accepted that if I just changed my mind to stop getting caught up in moments of failure, if I changed my *perspective*, I could change my trajectory and actually succeed in accomplishing my goals. So I started to look at my situation differently, and it propelled me to move forward.

Is the glass half full or half empty?

It's all about perspective! My perspective now is one of hope and optimism, and I want the same for you.

SECTION 3:
SELF-MOTIVATION

CHAPTER 6:
GETTING AND STAYING
MOTIVATED

Self-motivation is heartfelt. It's *why* you do what you do. It's what helps you commit.

If you desire a positive outcome, you can expect great things to happen– but only if you decide to take action. And taking action requires motivation.

If you're lazing on the couch and don't feel like moving, but manage to pull yourself up and go into the kitchen, it's probably because you were hungry– that hunger motivated you to grab a snack.

There are things you have to do on your own; action steps to take. Expecting great things to happen without taking action is futile. It's not going to be fulfilled. It's like holding your hand out, waiting in vain for treasures to fall from the sky.

Positive outcomes require commitment, strategic thinking, planning, and action.

By the way, you're not going to reach the finish line alone. The great thing I understand about achieving my goals is that

I can't succeed without help from other people. You do need to take action, but you don't achieve a goal all on your own. Someone or something is going to be there to help you accomplish that particular goal. In fact, if you take an inventory, you'll find there's no goal you've achieved without someone having helped you achieve it. That's how goals are designed.

Extrinsic and Intrinsic Motivations

Extrinsic motivation is knowing that when you accomplish certain things, it will allow you to get the *externals* you seek, whether it's a car, a house, etc.

Intrinsic motivation is more about personal satisfaction and fulfillment, or the internal rewards.

My own motivation to write this book was to not only give folks tools so they can help themselves but to help others as well, such as colleagues, etc.. I really care about what people go through emotionally, and knowing there are tools out there to help navigate that, it's important to me to be able to share these tools in a way that people can easily digest. This book is not designed to be a difficult read; these are simple, proven concepts that can slowly but surely help you shift your life in the right direction.

Extrinsic and intrinsic motivations are interconnected. And I think it's important to have a healthy balance of each.

When I was working in the business of sales, the focus was on, *Hey, if you sell this product or service, you're able to buy X and you're able to buy Z*. Well, if I'm only motivated by those material, external things, the inner self is not being fulfilled and it actually leaves one feeling empty.

But I also find that if I *only* focus on intrinsic motivations, then the external components may be left out. As a husband and father, I have a need to be a good provider, to take care of my house, to send my kids to school. And this all connects back to intrinsic motivation because being able to provide those externals gives me internal satisfaction as well.

The goal is to be able to have a balance because they're both important for a positive outcome of fulfillment. So I urge you to do a self-assessment to figure out what truly motivates you; both the external things you want, as well as what your inner person finds satisfying and meaningful.

Your spirit, *your unique spark*, is what really connects you to your big-picture motivation, keeping you inspired for the long haul.

CHAPTER 7:
SPIRITUALLY GROUNDED
AND FOCUSED

In this chapter I will share Bible quotes, inter-preting them as they can be applied to business matters– not to evangelize.

Back in 1989, I worked for Alamo Rent a Car where I had my first opportunity to become a manager.

I started as a rental car agent specialist. It became a very interesting role within a matter of weeks when the night supervisor was terminated for negligent activity.

Over the next few days, I assumed several people – who I assumed were naturals – would apply for the night supervisor position. But they didn't. I was surprised and shocked. I asked around, wondering why these people weren't applying for the role, and was simply told none of them were interested.

Granted, I was the newest person on the team, but I still decided to look at the job description to see what it entailed. Soon, I scheduled a meeting with the general manager to express my interest in the position. Sure enough, he offered me the job!

This is how I learned one of the keys, not only to self-confidence, but for leading others as well: **creating value**, no matter your current role. You may not have a lot of resources, like experience and skill (yet), but what's most important is to demonstrate your value. By stepping up and offering myself to fill a needed role, that's exactly what I had done.

I was very glad to get the promotion, but I had no idea how I was going to accomplish the duties of my new job– on top of that, I'd have to oversee people I'd just met as the newest hire! This would be a challenging situation to step into, and it encouraged me to remain spiritually connected and grounded, which is– another key principle. A biblical verse from Philippians 4:13 says: *I can do all things through Christ who strengthens me.* This quote has helped ground me throughout my career.

As a leader, I've found that providing guidance, direction, and clarity in helping to develop teams, as well as developing myself, requires a certain direction and spirit to help others see, and connect to, the bigger picture. I have to reach back to my younger self who reminds me it's okay to ask questions.

Being spiritually connected is a key component and ingredient that has helped me, and I encourage other leaders to embrace their spiritual side.

Three months into my new role, I realized I did not know what I *did know* about the job. To be able to accomplish the tasks set forth for me, I had a lot to learn. I had to summon strength in order to support the team I was to lead.

I often said, *"Hey, I don't have all the answers but I know we can figure it out together."*

This transparent attitude with my colleagues enabled me to build rapport with my team members, to meet them where they were, and to better understand what barriers or roadblocks they were facing.

And as I dove into a new level of understanding, committed to building relationships with my team members, *they* were more inclined to help *me* to be successful.

This is a very important component. You have to go into a management position prepared to lead people. **And it's okay to ask questions.**

Posing questions is an opportunity for leaders. Sometimes, those in leadership positions feel they don't want to ask questions, especially to their peer group, because they may be judged as knowing less than they should– perhaps less than their employees at times. However, as discussed earlier, the willingness to ask questions is actually a *strength*. Not only do I ask questions of my boss and my peers, I also ask questions of my employees because they're closer to the task at-hand and often have insights that I don't.

When Bad Things Happen

As I continued to learn and grow as a business leader, I worked for a wireless company by the name of MCI.

One of my employees, Nita, went out on a sales call to visit a company and she was able to win their business. I had to validate her sale, which I did to the best of my ability. A few days later, I received a call from my boss asking me if I had validated her sale.

I said, "Yes, I did it according to the protocol."

Well, the internal insight group did their own research, only to find out the deal was fraudulent. My manager told me I had missed the opportunity to correctly validate her sale and, because of this, I was going to be reprimanded with a document in my file saying that I "neglected to follow protocol." Because of that, I received the following warning: *If it should happen again, it could lead to further disciplinary action, up to and including termination.*

I was really appalled and challenged by this, especially since I had done everything by the book. Perhaps there was a mistake elsewhere? In addition, Nita was *not* reprimanded, only I was, as her supervisor.

I shared the story with family and friends. People on the team told me, "You did what you were supposed to do. They're treating you differently because of the color of your skin."

This perspective put me in a perplexing situation and I was careful about absorbing it, unsure what, if anything, I would do next. There's a great quote from Galatians 6:9 that sustained me through this: ***Let us not grow weary in well-doing, for in due season we shall reap, if we do not lose heart.***

Things Have a Way of Working Out

A few days after I received the write-up, I got another call from my manager. He said, "Richard, you did what you were supposed to do. The person who performed the oversight made a mistake. You were correct."

I also received an apologetic call from our VP of Sales.

When you know you're in the right, do not give up on yourself or a situation, however bad it may seem. Even when there have been conversations about my falling short of monthly goals or challenging situations like just described, my goal has always been to stay focused, remain disciplined, and view it as an opportunity to rise *above* the circumstances, to remain spiritually grounded and connected.

I believe, and my experiences have shown me, that if you do the right things for the right reasons, you can expect great things to happen.

If I had the opportunity to go back to my younger self and ask, "Richard, what is life going to be like?," I know my younger self was concerned. *What is my future going to look like? What am I going to grow up to be? What book will I write? What job will I have? Who will I marry?* So many uncertainties.

If I had a chance today to reassure myself at that age, I wouldn't have been worried or concerned. I would have the confidence and assurance that things are going to work out in my favor. Just reflecting on when I took the job in Alamo, I see that things have a way of working out. Even with everything I'm working on now, I can reflect on my younger self and look at my track record, my history, my experiences, and see that even the most volatile ones still worked out in my favor, to my benefit. I believe all things are designed to be that way.

Making Tough Choices

In 2014, I was traveling weekly to Albuquerque, New Mexico for a temporary assignment around a new opportunity. I was asked to step in for another director for a couple of months. The assignment was imposed on me without my consent, and became extended for much longer than I had expected.

Once we were acquired by AT&T, I was asked if I would be interested in fulfilling this role *permanently* in Albuquerque. I said, "Thank you, but no, thank you. My family and I really enjoy living in Southern California."

Based on my decision, my boss, as well as the HR folks, shared with me that I would be placed on their "surplus list." That meant I had 60 days to find a new role. If I could not find a new role in San Diego within Cricket Wireless or AT&T, I would be relieved of my employment.

There were some benefits to being on the surplus list. If I did not find a new role within the company, my stock options would become vested immediately. I ended up leaving and received a solid severance package, which gave me the opportunity to start my own company: RDM Management Group.

At the time, I had no clue what it would actually take – the focus, discipline and tenacity – required to start my own business. I was leaving a stable environment where I was the Director of Sales to become an entrepreneur and establish a training company.

Proverbs 3:5-6 says, *"Trust in the Lord with all your heart and lean not on your own understanding; in all your ways submit to him, and he will make your paths straight."*

So, rather than 'lean only on my own understanding,' I asked for direction and guidance.

Entrepreneurship can be challenging. Remaining focused and disciplined and spiritually grounded has allowed me to experience things in life that I had previously only dreamed about. This is the key to becoming the best version of yourself that you can possibly be. I would like to encourage you to stay focused, stay disciplined, and know that all things are possible. If you believe that, if you stretch beyond yourself, expect great things to happen.

Do Unto Others as You Would Have Others Do Unto You

In the big picture, *do unto others as you would have them do unto you* is a universal spiritual principle. It's also a useful motivator in business. By treating customers and colleagues with dignity and respect, being truthful, being transparent, and helping them accomplish their goals, you automatically get what is coming to you, which is your goal to build business, grow revenue, etc.

A healthy motivation is doing the right things for the right reasons in the moment, as opposed to manipulation or playing a shell game. Trying to manipulate or take advantage of customers or staff members doesn't work well and it's definitely not sustainable.

Show people you care about them, not just verbally, but with your actions. In your conversations, be mentally present as people share with you what may be their innermost thoughts. Be compassionate. Showing compassion to your team members will go a long way. It's as simple as communicating that you care about them, through displaying empathy, and through telling them that you care. We will explore this topic further in Section 5: Emotional Intelligence.

Be transparent, let your team know that you're human, and a 'work under construction.' Just because you're in a leadership position doesn't mean that you're not working on yourself too, and you can learn and grow and benefit together, *as a team.*

Not only does this approach foster a more pleasant work environment, your care for employees directly impacts their productivity, which directly impacts your company's profitability.

A friend of mine once told me, "There *is* an 'I' in team. The 'I' represents each 'individual' on the team, meaning that if an individual doesn't do his or her part, a team cannot be successful."

I am asking you, the reader, to do your *individual* part.

Whether you're an employee, a consultant, a manager, department head, or CEO, be the best person you can possibly be, as an individual. Tap into the *Inner You*– your inner strength and tenacity and resilience. Share with others, and care for others.

It's not just a leader's responsibility, it's our responsibility to each other, as individuals. This book is meant to encourage you to be the best person you can possibly become, and not just in business.

What if there are no accidents? Perhaps you have an assignment, to be a positive influence and have a positive impact on the people you know and work with– and what if this positive influence ripples to the people they know as well? Every interaction is an opportunity to deposit something that is positive.

I encourage you to surround yourself with positive people and to encourage them to be the best version of themselves, too. I charge all of us to be the best version of ourselves. Not only to help ourselves, but to be helpful to the other people in our lives.

SECTION 4:
SELF-DISCIPLINE

CHAPTER 8:
SELF-MANAGEMENT

The second component of emotional intelligence, as defined by Travis Bradberry, is self-management, which is about self-regulation and how we manage ourselves.

Self-management is about self-discipline, it's about developing better control over our own impulses and our quick judgments about others. I know many of us could improve in this area. It's not about being in total control of your thoughts and actions every minute of the day because that's just not realistic, or even possible. It's about doing your best with what you know, and having the willingness to grow.

Self-management is the ability to control or redirect disruptive impulses, like bad moods, and to suspend judgment, that is, to **think before you act**. The ability to control one's self from automatic reactions can be challenging. As I interact with many leaders across the world, one of the areas that many of them say they need to work on is patience, including patience for others in their organization who are not as disciplined as they are, or who fall short of their own expectations.

When people fall short of my expectations, I admit that I too can feel impatient. But when I react to my impatience, chances are that you will see the stress and anxiety on my face. I can become short with people, and speak in a very matter-of-fact tone which can come across as cold, creating additional stress and anxiety for those who work for me. The negative impact my mood can have on other people is a **result** of a lack of self-management.

Rushing to judgment is another example of lacking self-management. When I was a kid, I was told, "Never judge a book by its cover." Most of us were taught these words of wisdom growing up, but when you lack self-management you may be unable to actually follow them.

For example, when I have set my expectations and others fall short of meeting them, chances are that I will start judging them by my perception of their performance – judging that book by its cover. I could call them lazy or uncommitted, or complain, "So and so failed to meet *my* expectations."

However, chances are that I need to suspend my judgment slightly, so I can meet them where they are; meaning, take the time to understand how they're responding to their engagement with me and the tasks I've set.

One way to avoid "judging a book by its cover," in this case, is to look at their assignments from their perspective. It's possible that what I thought was a realistic timeframe to complete a task was not all that realistic. Even if it was, I'm likely to get better results going forward if I manage *myself* before confronting them about missing a deadline.

To think before you act is so important. If I use self-management, I'm better able to maintain my self-discipline and patience, and remain more in control of myself, so that I have the ability to clearly think through my actions *before* I act. If I berate them, if I humiliate them, if I behave irresponsibly in the workplace, chances are I didn't think through my response. This is a clear sign that I'm not practicing self-management.

It also goes back to self-awareness: understanding how my mood and words and actions are impacting the people around me, and especially how they're working for me.

CHAPTER 9:
GROWTH MINDSET

I was first introduced to the idea of having a "Growth Mindset" many years ago.

As I researched this concept, I thought it would be a good thing to introduce to my adult learners. My instinct was to share it with my students as a way for them to learn what it means to grow their minds, to shift out of stagnant ideas, to explore unlimited possibilities, and to accept the ironies of life. It's also a valuable form of self-discipline.

As I was teaching Growth Mindset, I began to apply it to my own personal life, and it took on a different shape and format.

The idea of the Growth Mindset has been around for years. It was introduced by American psychologist and researcher, Dr. Carol Dweck, who has several publications explaining her theories.

The Growth Mindset is viewing any situation, especially difficult situations, as an opportunity for you to learn, grow, and change for the better, by focusing your attention on *improving yourself* rather than *changing yourself*, or **blaming anyone else**. I tell you, this was challenging for me.

So, I ask my readers to do an internal assessment. Take a look at any situation you currently find yourself in, especially a difficult one. Now think of this situation as an opportunity for you to learn something valuable. ***What can you learn from that situation?***

If you're anything like me, you may find this easier said than done. The last thing I wanted to do was learn. My thought process was usually, *I just want to get the heck out of this situation.*

The Growth Mindset also challenges us to **grow** from the difficult situations we find ourselves in, which is complex all on its own. *What have I done to learn and grow from my challenging situations?*

Not wanting to do this work, I can understand. Would anyone rather have a beer right now?

What helped me overcome my own resistance was my willingness to get myself into a better situation.

When I was a kid, I was told that people do not like change. I grew up not liking change and I've seen that most people don't. As I grew and matured, I started to realize that change is one of the things that is a constant in life. There is no avoiding it.

Part of this topic is focusing attention on improving yourself. I personally do not have a problem with that. Blaming others or trying to change them to fix my own situation did not resonate with me. But looking at my close relationships – coworkers, friends, and relatives – I realized I had a tendency to think, *You have got to get yourself together, this is your problem. Life would be so much better for me if you would just change.* Having other people in my life change and fix themselves will make life a hell of a lot better for all concerned.

That's not a Growth Mindset. The Growth Mindset involves focusing my attention on improving myself instead of blaming others.

I know now that I *cannot* change other people. What I *can* change is my perspective. That's what the Growth Mindset does. It allows you to grow and mature and challenge yourself. The Growth Mindset has allowed me to become the best version of myself that I can possibly be while still learning, growing, and expanding in all that I do.

I can fly and soar towards the destiny I have chosen, because the choice is ours, and a Growth Mindset provides the opportunity to do that.

Limitations of a Fixed Mindset

Many of us bounce between a Fixed Mindset and a Growth Mindset.

There are some people who would think or say things like, "I'm either good at it or I'm not."

This type of either/or thinking creates self-limiting options; *I can only see two possibilities.* If we're struggling to learn something new and get easily frustrated and quickly give up, we're thereby limiting our own potential growth.

I don't like to be challenged is another limiting perspective. This type of mindset is that of someone who would rather stay stuck than try something new. This person may choose to stay in a status quo for a long period of time, even if they don't like it.

When I fail, I'm no good. This is an emotional state that happens to us all. And I've devolved into that category plenty of times. However, I do not stay there, and *that* is what's important.

The difference between a Fixed Mindset person and a Growth Mindset person is that the Growth Mindset person says, "I failed this time, but I still learned something," versus the Fixed Mindset person who may think, "I'm just no good," or "I'll never be good at this."

A Fixed Mindset person may want to be told that they're smart. A Growth Mindset person is more focused on increasing their knowledge.

A few years ago, I was conducting a Growth Mindset training and the room was full of managers and their employees. One particular manager admitted, "If you succeed, I feel threatened."

Keep in mind that his employees were in the room when he made this statement. It was eye-opening for them because whenever they brought him a new idea, he was not receptive and he would not accept it. Instead, he would shoot down their ideas like they were fish in a barrel. Now they knew why– it was because he felt *threatened*.

A Fixed Mindset doesn't just impact you, it impacts everyone who is under your influence. If you're not willing to learn and grow and change, you are limiting yourself. And you are most definitely having a limiting effect on your subordinates.

As leaders, we must do better! We must grow out of our fixed mindsets. If you can cultivate a Growth Mindset, you will not only expand your own possibilities, but you will also become an inspiration to others.

Unconscious Bias Leads to a Fixed Mindset

A client of mine told me they were having difficulty integrating new employees who had recently graduated from college. There were a lot of baby boomers working there who wouldn't give the younger employees a chance. They weren't inclined to coach them or nurture them or help them develop. Because of that, the company was experiencing a 40% attrition rate among the new employees – they didn't feel welcomed because of the older crowd's biases toward them.

To me, that is a big missed opportunity and an example of having a Closed Mindset.

Taking people on an individual basis instead of judging them on one or more of their characteristics, giving them a chance, learning about them and their strengths, talking honestly about differences, embracing and even celebrating those differences–this all comes from a Growth Mindset.

What Type of Mindset Do You Have?

The Growth Mindset offers limitless opportunities. You can learn anything. "Yes, I can," says the Growth Mindset person.

If there's something they want to achieve, they convince themselves that they are capable of learning what they need to learn. They don't let their frustrations get the better of them when they run into barriers or roadblocks. Instead, they figure out a way around or over them.

When I'm frustrated, I persevere. Yes, it impacts me emotionally. Yes, I feel the pain of frustration. Instead of wallowing in those feelings, I get up and figure out how to get myself out of the situation or circumstances so that I may achieve my desired outcome.

The Growth Mindset person says, "I like a challenge."

The status quo is not good enough. He or she navigates and keeps moving through life's complexities, toward their ultimate greatness and success.

"When I fail, I learn," says the Growth Mindset person.

Over time, he or she begins to understand that failure is actually the road to success. It's impossible to have success without failure. The more I fail, the more I put myself in a position to succeed.

"My efforts and attitude determine everything," says the Growth Mindset person.

They have a vision and a goal. They have an objective to accomplish. They have dreams to pursue for their life and their happiness and to enjoy the world. Focusing on the results they want to achieve fills them with energy and puts them in alignment to be able to overcome any complexities.

Yes, life can be difficult. Life will be challenging. The Growth Mindset person stays motivated and perseveres by learning from their experiences, bettering themselves, and putting in the necessary effort to accomplish their goals. They expect great things to happen, and great things often do.

Here's an example from my own life on how the shift from a fixed mindset to a growth mindset can work.

When I was working for a wireless carrier, my leader at the time, Randy, trusted me with the organization. He said, "Richard, I'm giving you keys to the castle. Run it as you see fit and update me in our weekly one-on-one."

Soon after, he went on a two-week vacation. While he was gone, I made a few decisions. When he returned, I updated him, and when I was sharing the decisions I'd made, he said, "Hold it, Cowboy, you need to reign that one back in."

I'm like, *What do you mean?*

He continued, "That decision you just made about 'X'; we need to change it. You need to put it back the way it was. Meet with your team and tell them we're going in a different direction."

I asked him, "Why do I need to do that? You trust me, I did it, and it's actually being worked out as we speak."

He said, "I understand that, but we need to go in a different direction."

I pushed back because I thought my decision-making was being challenged and it frustrated me. I'm thinking, *If I go back to my team and they know Randy is back from vacation and I just had a one-on-one with him, they're going to assume I make bad decisions on my own without my boss.*

I didn't want to lose face with my team, so I believed I needed to stand up for my decision. As I began to do that, Randy got really direct and to the point. "No. We need to go in this different direction."

Honestly, it pissed me off and I became somewhat argumentative. Long story short, I walked out of his office to return to my office and I closed his door just a little too loudly.

He got out of his chair, walked over to my desk and said, "Richard, you're on the verge of being insubordinate. What is going on with you? Just do what I ask, and do it now."

I said, "Yes, sir."

I called my team and said that we needed to have a conference call. I explained to them that we had to change direction and they said, "Okay, no problem."

They were easy about it, but I was still annoyed. Remember, ego is one of the top two causes of human suffering.

I just didn't like the idea of having to change my leadership decision. So that evening I talked to my wife, venting about the situation. But she didn't see it as a big deal– this, of course, frustrated me even more. I wanted to do what I wanted to do, and I believed my decision was the right one.

I went into the office for the next couple of days and my conversations with Randy were minimal. I was being respectful, but I didn't want to have too much interaction. That Friday, I was still frustrated. Saturday, still frustrated. On Sunday, I turned on the TV to see Joel Osteen, a well-known pastor in Houston, who, ironically enough, was talking about how when leaders or bosses and employees have conflict, one of the primary reasons is because the leader wants to go one direction and the employee wants to go in a different direction in terms of achieving their organization or team's goals and outcomes.

That caught my attention. *Yes! I want to go one way; he wants to go another.* Like it or not, I have to submit because he's the boss.

The second thing he said was that we need to be able to **manage our behavior**. He said, do you think your boss in this situation is equally upset? Do you think he's at home frustrated, still talking about it?

I knew Randy and I realized, *No, he's not thinking about this.* But I still am and it's been plaguing me for an entire week.

Joel Osteen said that we, as Christians, should be able to submit to authority, as long as it's correct and not putting us in harm's way. We also need to think about the fact that even though this may be a difficult experience, it may not be that bad. Does it really have to continue as difficult conversations and head-butting, or could this possibly work out to your benefit?

By changing your perspective, maybe you could change your expectations. *Instead of expecting difficult things to continue with this relationship, can you expect something positive?*

What can you learn from this, and how can you grow?

A seed was planted. I didn't want an ongoing horrible relationship with my boss. My desired outcome was positive, even though I couldn't yet see how it could come about from my current perspective. I began to consider that, even in this frustrating situation, something good could possibly come of it.

My perspective was shifting and that Monday when I went back to the office, I asked for a meeting. I apologized for being on the cusp of being disrespectful, for being frustrated, and caught up in my own emotions.

Randy said, "I'm glad you came to that epiphany, because number one, if we would have stayed in that trajectory with the decision you made, it was going to have a negative impact on your employees. What you didn't know is that we're going to have a reduction and if you would have kept on in that direction, you would have lost fifty percent of your team instead of ten percent. So, that route would have had you losing more people." He added, "Number two, I'm glad you apologized for behaving disrespectfully."

Guess what? Randy became my best friend. We played racquetball together and everything. He became my advocate at work and I actually got promoted a couple of times under his leadership. All because I changed my perspective and attitude.

CHAPTER 10:
CULTIVATE SELF-DISCIPLINE

Self-awareness, self-confidence, and self-motivation are building blocks to enable and empower your self-discipline. Reaching worthwhile goals and achieving positive outcomes takes commitment, and commitment is what powers self-discipline.

Self-discipline means having the ability to discipline yourself rather than relying on outside pressure and/or encouragement to "make" you get things done.

As you develop more understanding of your attitudes, ego, and blind spots through increased self-awareness, you will need some self-discipline to apply what you learn, as discussed earlier in the Self-Management chapter.

Self-discipline means making those tough decisions to do what you don't want to do or feel like doing, but that you *need* to do in order to accomplish the things you seek.

As a minor example, you may not feel like going to the dry cleaners, but you feel confident in your favorite power suit and want to wear it to an important upcoming meeting, so you take the steps to get it cleaned in time for the meeting.

It can be about working longer hours, going above and beyond to make a positive impression. It's about integrity, honoring your commitments to yourself and others.

It's also about saying "no" to things that are counterproductive to your desired outcomes.

Motivation and Discipline Work Together

Self-discipline, supported by self-motivation to stay focused on accomplishing your goals, helps you push through your own resistance and keeps you on track. Even if you don't feel like doing something, you want to move away from disappointing yourself, by moving away from the habits and other things that are detrimental to your goals.

I found that most of us know what to do and we know what not to do. Whether it's weight loss or accomplishing any other goals. You identify the things you'd like to achieve, and once you've done the research, you actually know what you need to do.

Taking the appropriate actions and actually *doing* those things is another matter. Sometimes I do something polar opposite, because being disciplined can be an inconvenience. I want to do what's fun right now. I want to do what's comfortable. Sometimes we instinctively do the things we know we shouldn't be doing because they're counterproductive to our desired outcomes. We all know it takes discipline to break bad habits. Being disciplined at times forces us to find a way to get comfortable with being uncomfortable, for the sake of our big picture goals.

But self-discipline alone is not going to work well or be sustainable without having the right motivations – the ones that truly motivate us. Remember, we have both intrinsic and extrinsic motivations and it's ideal to have a good balance of both.

Having motivation without discipline is not going to work either. Our goals and outcomes are interconnected. Discipline is the bridge to the positive outcome, whether personal or professional.

Self-discipline is especially important in a leadership role. If you're not a person of your word and if you don't follow through on your commitments, you're going to have a hard time convincing anyone to trust you with increasing responsibility. You're also going to find it difficult, if not impossible, to lead others effectively.

SECTION 5:
EMOTIONAL INTELLIGENCE

CHAPTER 11:
IQ VS EQ

IQ versus EQ – these are key components that often get confused, even by leaders.

IQ, also known as Intelligence Quotient, is a score derived from a series of standardized tests designed to assess intelligence – how smart you are; your ability to learn, understand, and apply information skills such as logical reasoning, word comprehension, and math skills. It also includes abstract and spatial thinking, which are more relative skills that you and I also need in business and in life.

In the workplace, your Intelligence Quotient shows up as success in completing challenging tasks, the aptitude to analyze data, and the reasoning ability to "connect the dots," as is often needed in research and development.

In my training class, I ask audience members to share what it is that they do for a living. They describe their job titles and their job description, which is the outlier of their Intelligence Quotient. Often it is our hard skills that allow us to be effective in our roles within the workplace.

Typically, when a person is promoted from individual contributor to leader, he or she is promoted based on a hard skill or a set of skills that they were able to demonstrate consistently, allowing them to do their job well. That is, pulling from their Intelligence Quotient, or IQ.

However, as we transition into a leadership role, IQ alone will not sustain us.. Intelligence Quotient (IQ) cannot be abandoned when we grow into leadership roles and responsibilities, but we most definitely need to incorporate and embrace additional skills as well. As I work with many leaders across this country, I've found that many of them are totally unaware of their blind spots that interfere with their own effectiveness and leadership potential.

I had a client who is an engineer. A very smart individual who was able to successfully grow his career based on that hard skill. He works in the technical arena so his IQ is really important.

As he took on his new leadership role, he began to make very aggressive changes – changes that his own manager had even asked for him to address, and he did so with the best of intentions. But he did *not* take into account the impact his changes were going to have on his direct reports.

So, he was a new leader of a team and he came in with his changes. Not only did he change the processes but he also spoke ill of the current processes that were in place. He would say things like, "What were they thinking, putting these processes and procedures in place?" and "Did they not understand how this was going to negatively impact the business?"

What he failed to realize was that many of the people he was complaining to, who were now working under him, were the same people who had initially created the strategic processes and procedures he was so eagerly planning to replace.

Granted that his decisions were sound – they were improvements that needed to take place and he knew how to make them, but along the way he offended the people who had made those decisions prior to his arrival as the new leader of their team.

Perhaps there was some other way he could have addressed the issues and introduced his changes?

He could have asked questions like, "Who created this policy? What is the reasoning behind this procedure? What allowed us to create these processes?"

Even, "What was it like (in this department) back then?" and "What impact did it have on our business when these procedures were first put into practice?" would have been good questions to ask.

Business is a moving target because what worked in the past is not necessarily what is going to work moving forward. As this engineer took over his new responsibilities, his inability to display curiosity about decisions that were made prior to his arrival, coupled with not being consciously aware of how his mood and actions would impact the people he was working with, are a perfect example of a person with a high IQ but a low EQ.

What is EQ?

EQ stands for "Emotional Quotient" and is also known as "Emotional Intelligence."

Emotional Intelligence is an awareness of people's *emotional* side. It's the ability to identify, assess, and, as needed, control one's own emotions– that is, to manage how they are expressed.

For example, rather than knee-jerk responses to something going wrong, a person with Emotional Intelligence is more likely to take into account how an individual or group might respond to an angry outburst. So it also means having awareness of, and empathy for, the emotions and potential responses of others. As in the above example, blanket criticism for someone's past work is likely to put them on the defensive, whereas explaining how and why the original approach is being changed and upgraded, even seeking input on how best to implement the changes, is likely to elicit a much more beneficial response. That takes Emotional Intelligence.

The Difference Between Sympathy and Empathy

Sympathy is the feeling of caring or "giving a crap" for something or someone– it's feeling sorry to see someone's trouble, grief, or misfortune. It can also mean feeling supportive of something, and when people share common interests, opinions, or goals you can say they are in sympathy with each other.

Empathy is similar to sympathy in that it has to do with caring about others, but it goes a step further. Empathy is the ability to truly put yourself in someone else's shoes so that you can accurately assess how they feel and meet them where they are. It's understanding, being aware of, being sensitive to, even experiencing the feelings, thoughts, and experiences of another.

Perceiving and assessing others' potential emotions helps you understand, "where they're coming from" and enables you to facilitate more productive thinking, action, and teamwork.

An Empathetic Leader

I believe emotionally intelligent leaders understand the importance of the impact that their comments, their views or perspectives, and their own emotions have on other people, whether they're direct reports on their own team or people who operate somewhere within their sphere of influence.

This is a skillset, and being unaware of the impact of your own thoughts, feelings and words, and how you express them, can have a gravely unfavorable impact on the people you want to influence the most. As someone in a leadership position, the intent of your role in the workplace is for you to effectively guide and motivate each member of your team, helping them to navigate challenges and work together harmoniously– even when individuals are at odds with one another or other departments.

Positively influencing people with emotional intelligence in leadership starts with understanding how your own mood and actions will impact others. Your level of ability to communicate will be demonstrated in successful relationships with others.

Contrary to popular belief, being a leader doesn't mean bossing people around. It means being service-oriented and setting an example for how to properly communicate, for the greater good of both your team and your company as a whole. As a leader, it is actually your role and responsibility to serve not just the clients who have decided to spend time with your organization, but each team member and direct report as well.

Have you worked for, or with, people in which your interaction with them would suggest that they're talented, brilliant, smart people who know how to get the job done, but who have no people skills? That's what Emotional Intelligence is: *people skills*. And this includes the ability to communicate <u>effectively</u>.

You see, Emotional Intelligence doesn't out-trump Intelligence Quotient (IQ) but it makes a world of difference when it comes to interacting with others, which is unavoidable in business, and in life.

I remember working with a senior leader at an organization who was very smart. He knew how to generate revenue, but if you placed him in front of an audience he would falter very quickly. He did not have the ability to share empathy with the audience, and he had a challenge in being able to understand where other people were coming from. He was so practical and pragmatic and, even though it wasn't his intent, his conversation often offended people. We ought to have to measure intent versus outcome, we would learn a lot.

Often the intent is, *I want to be successful in delivering my message and I want to be able to help people understand what they need to understand, so I can actually drive them in the right direction, to the results our organization is after.* But the outcome will fall short of the goal if I did not properly incorporate Emotional Intelligence.

Regardless of where you are today with this very important topic of Emotional Intelligence, you can always improve with focus and discipline. Considering the feelings of others and building effective communication are skill sets that can be learned.

Keep in mind that Emotion Intelligence is something that is in each of us, even if it's currently dormant. It's intangible, meaning you can't touch it and it's hard to measure– but know that it is there. It affects how we manage our own behavior as well as the potential responses and behavior of others. It's about navigating social complexities. The more challenging and difficult the situation, the greater the opportunity to make use of Emotional Intelligence to make personal decisions that achieve positive results.

As we interact with each other, as we navigate through complexities, if the outcome is not positive or what you would have wished, it may be an area of opportunity for practicing the skills of Emotional Intelligence. Again, it is the ability to recognize and understand emotions in yourself and others.

This requires patience and listening, which are skill sets that can be practiced. In order to communicate effectively and strategically, you need both self-awareness and awareness of others to help you manage your own behavior and your relationships.

CHAPTER 12:
DEVELOPING EQ

As previously discussed in Section One, Travis Bradberry's first category of Emotional Intelligence is self-awareness.

The negative impact of a lack of self-awareness is multiplied when I'm interacting with team members. As a leader, good, bad, or indifferent, I am setting the stage for people to follow. I am the one leading by example and, because of that, I need to be consciously aware of the example I'm setting for others.

Being able to communicate directly and assertively is so important. Assertive communication is that sweet spot between aggressive and passive-aggressive. Just because you're able to tell people what you think and what's on your mind, that doesn't mean you're doing it in an effective way. If you do that without taking into account the potential impact, chances are you can easily offend someone, albeit unintentionally.

Being direct doesn't always mean you're doing it in the "emotional intelligence way," meaning, if you are communicating directly with your audience or your team members or others, and they feel like they've been taken advantage of, like they've been hit in the face by a verbal assault, chances are you're not practicing Emotional Intelligence.

In other words, you don't automatically understand the impact of your lack of self-awareness and how your moods and actions are impacting other people. If the outcome is negative, or counter to your desired outcome, it may be an area of opportunity to increase your self-awareness.

Ego and Blind Spots at Work

The ego is our attitude, our viewpoint, our sense of self. We don't want to be wrong and because we don't want to be wrong, our egos get in the way which creates a divide – an issue that especially impacts social skills and the ability to build rapport with others.

Remember my conflict with Randy? I didn't want to be wrong, especially in front of my team. Granted, I didn't have all the information he had; but my ego about it caused our rapport to break down until I came around.

Another side of ego at work is this belief: *I have to do it all myself, and/or I'm the only one who can do this task correctly.* We must learn to set our ego aside and allow ourselves to ask for help, and also to delegate. This allows us to develop our people to be self-reliant employees and, eventually, leaders themselves.

Our blind spots can cause us a lot of problems in the workplace. Because of those blind spots, we can't stop ourselves from making certain harmful mistakes until we go through a process to increase our self-awareness, and by then, it may be too late to correct a problem.

In 20/20 hindsight, we can see our past mistakes more clearly and the impact of our past actions, as well as those of others, and better understand the differing narrative or points of view of different people, or even departments.

But if we're unable to forgive others' past mistakes so that we can build on and improve our working relationships, worse mistakes may be made – mistakes that could become patterns because we didn't learn from them. We still don't know what we did not know.

Social Awareness

Travis Bradberry's third component of Emotional Intelligence is Social Awareness. Social awareness is the ability to understand the emotional makeup of a group of other people. Social awareness is simply showing empathy to a demographic (religious group, political group, ethnic group, gender group, etc.) that is different from one's own.

Social awareness allows you to meet people where they are, respectfully. This often means I need to have less of myself showing up in the conversation, including my opinions, judgements, and biases.

Wouldn't it be great if our country did a better job with social awareness?

As I listen to political rhetoric, quite often there is a large gap, not only between politicians and parties, but between politicians and the people they are meant to serve.

I purposely listen to both Democratic and Republican news stations, and it's amazing to find two completely different narratives that are polarizing; pushing their viewers and listeners to more and more extreme positions, thereby forcing audiences to "choose a side." As listeners' perspectives are shaped by these polarizing views, it creates a blanket lack of empathy for anyone on "the other side" – *and* a diminishing of overall Emotional Intelligence. That's not healthy or productive for a society, and it's not how life works for many of us.

We are in a climate now that suggests that this lack of social awareness and empathy for one another is creating social unrest. When we fail to display empathy for another group or person, it's as if telling them, *"I don't care about you and I don't value you."*

That doesn't go over very well with the person or group on the receiving end of that message.

If someone consistently receives that same message, it is almost like a denial of their humanity, and they are eventually going to resist, and even act out their resistance in some form or fashion.

In the social environment, it expresses as push back in the form of social unrest – protests, riots, uprisings.

In the workplace, it can show up as low morale, lack of focus, reduced productivity, and, possibly, "phoning it in" as they seek a new job.

Empathy is communicating and actively demonstrating this sentiment: *I care about you and I expect you to care about me, too.*

Imagine what it would be like around the country and around the globe if we were able to display empathy and demonstrate that we care for our fellow human beings. What if we cared for and valued each other, regardless of our differences?

We don't have to agree, but it's important to cultivate respect for one another regardless of our differences. *"I care about you simply because you're a human being,"* has the power to unite us rather than divide us – both as a nation and in the workplace.

Empathy in the Workplace

Healthy, productive business and personal relations are all about collaboration and understanding others– and both require empathy.

Empathy is caring for people. It's a natural human experience and we're all capable of expressing it. In corporate America, however, at least early in my career, caring was deemed as a weakness. The message was, *You don't need to show them you care, they need to go and do what you hired them to do. Just tell them to get the job done.*

I found that leaders who manage this way eventually run into a lot of problems with their staff, because they become unrelatable. When there's a communication breakdown between the employee and the employer, the employee says things like, "I can't talk to my leader."

The outcome is that their leader misses out on important information that they need in order to lead effectively.

Unfortunately, there is a major Emotional Intelligence gap with many leaders that directly interferes with their leadership ability.

These individuals often believe that if you care about a person and if you communicate that you care, it's a display of weakness. Many leaders believe they will be judged harshly by their own supervisors for not being tough enough and for being unable to "draw down the hammer" to get things done.

But that's simply not the case. As I survey employees across the land, it is always when empathy is absent that they develop a bad attitude toward their job, and their output suffers. Their leader may be able to prevail upon them to execute tasks and get the job done, but the leader's lack of interpersonal skills always carries a cost to both morale and productivity.

I used to think that these kinds of leaders were just, you know, jerks. What I've learned is that one of the primary reasons for their lack of empathy for employees is their lack of experience being treated with empathy themselves. They don't know how to apply "soft" skills, interpersonal skills.

Empathy is a skill you can develop and is a large part of emotional intelligence, but it's a process. Interpersonal skills can definitely be learned when you practice and apply listening and natural human caring.

What's so horrible about a leader letting their employee know that he or she cares about them? Leaders have been told that if you show your employees that you care, they're going to take advantage of that and they're going to misuse it. Granted, you could have some outliers, but you can deal with those accordingly.

As leaders, listening to the people who work for us is actually crucial to doing the job well. Yes, this could be viewed as relinquishing your power and control. I've found by relinquishing power over someone to be able to meet them where they are and listen to what they have to say, unconditionally, has allowed me to learn not only what's important to them, but also, often, something important for the department or even the company. At the same time, I was demonstrating that I cared, which increased our trust and rapport.

While working in corporate America, my goal was to know my team members so well that if they walked into someone's office, I could read the clues and discern immediately if something was going on with them that was interfering with their ability to stay focused and disciplined, or just counterproductive to the desired outcomes for their work, such as meeting sales goals.

I would ask a very simple question, and if I sensed something was off or out of the ordinary in their response, I would ask, "Excuse me, hey, are you okay?"

How they decided to respond was completely up to them, in terms of how candidly they communicated what was wrong, or if they answered the question at all. What I found was that my ability to sense they might be feeling troubled and simply ask sincerely if someone was okay, communicated that I cared about their wellbeing. That laid the foundation for a great bond and relationship between myself and the people who reported directly to me, as well as other co-workers and bosses.

I've surveyed many employees who perform a variety of different roles in the corporate space and I ask them, "What are the characteristics demonstrated by great leaders and people of influence?"

I most often hear words like, *"trust"*, *"vulnerability"*, *"empathy"*, and *"showing that he or she cares about me."*

Then I ask, "When did you know a manager or supervisor cared about you? How did that make you feel?"

These employees felt valued and appreciated by their leadership because of their displays of empathy, and it made the employees care about their leaders. Mutual empathy builds trust and transparency.

So, I encourage leaders to get to know your employees, listen to them, and understand what's important to them. Naturally and organically, this will build trust and transparency, while minimizing micromanaging, if not eradicating it completely. By showing the person that you care, that you trust them and appreciate them, it creates a sense of obligation. That worker thinks, *Because my leader cares about me personally, I'm going to go above and beyond for them.* They're motivated to accomplish any goals their leader assigns to them. That's what happens most of the time.

But if their leader doesn't show any level of concern or empathy, the employee thinks you don't care. Think about how we ourselves act when we believe someone doesn't care about us. Are you going to put your best foot forward? Nope. Are you going to go above and beyond? Nope. You just don't feel motivated because you assume, probably correctly, that your extra efforts won't be acknowledged or appreciated by someone who doesn't care about you.

The real reason you have to micromanage is that you can't trust employees to tell you if there's an issue or a problem. If the employee feels as though they can't come to you and share what's going on, there's going to be a delay in you learning something you need to know. They will eventually share it with you, but it's going to take a while for them to digest and figure out how they're going to communicate to you. They're thinking, *I don't want my manager to get angry or frustrated with me, so I need to think of a way to deliver this message.*

They might first talk to a family member, a friend, a coworker, maybe even another leader who seems more understanding. This delays your ability to identify what's going on with this employee and address the problem.

As a leader, obviously it behooves you to identify and address any issue as early as possible. One of the ways to do that is to build trust and rapport with your employees.

For an employee, not being micromanaged or having someone always looking over your shoulder is evidence of their leader's trust in them. In my experience, if an employee feels comfortable with you, trusted, valued, and respected, they will offer the same, and let you know immediately if there's something to report, even if it's unpleasant.

The people who work for a company are sometimes referred to as "human capital." If you're a leader and you can recognize people as your most important and valuable assets, you can become inspired to communicate effectively, develop your soft skills, show that you care, and generally invest in your relationships with them. You will be amazed at the results.

SECTION 6:
PUTTING IT ALL TOGETHER
APPLY THE FIVE TOOLS FOR
SUCCESS

CHAPTER 13:
INTERPERSONAL SKILLS

With a combination of self-awareness, self-confidence, self-motivation, and self-discipline, you have all the building blocks you need to build not only a successful career, but a fulfilling life.

Nothing is accomplished in a vacuum. People need people. By simply engaging your natural human ability to care about others and *show* that you care can take you to a whole other level. For many, developing their emotional intelligence may take embracing change and practicing interpersonal skills.

Interpersonal skills give a person the ability to interact with others harmoniously and successfully.

How you perceive my interaction with you is the result of my interpersonal skills, or lack of them. When you were speaking to me, could you tell if I was listening? Did you feel heard and understood? Or did you feel ignored, dismissed, or judged?

Social Skills

Travis Bradberry's fourth component of Emotional Intelligence is Social Skills – which is another way of saying *Interpersonal* Skills.

Social skills, developing rapport, managing relationships, and building networks are all huge parts of working in corporate America. An inability to find common ground with a variety of other people can severely undermine your potential for business success.

Interpersonal skills are what I call "power skills." They allow you to cultivate a calm, empathetic, and exceptional leadership ability.

Good interpersonal skills have a direct positive impact on critical thinking because they allow you to take in a variety of information from different sources. They also allow for more positivity and optimism – it is so much more relaxing and pleasant to get along with others than to constantly be at odds.

Interpersonal skills are quite important in business because different companies and different departments within a company are dependent on one another. Interpersonal skills are what give you the ability to connect with your coworkers. They give you the ability to connect with your boss or manager. They give you the ability to connect with your staff members.

It's imperative that the communication is fluid up and down the food chain. However, quite often, it gets stuck. Creativity and creative solutions are lost when communication is choked off in certain areas of an organization.

I was a witness to this dynamic throughout my business career, so I made it a personal goal to be able to connect, to the best of my ability, with every single person in the company.

If we are unable to listen objectively to what's being communicated, if we refuse to understand various people, or we insist on everything being done our own way instead of considering and incorporating others' thoughts and ideas, we are likely to create a disconnect. When that happens, it is interpersonal skills alone that will allow you to reconnect with people you feel alienated from, or who feel alienated from you.

There are times when, even if we disagree, we may have to do things in alignment with our leader's wishes, and/or policy and procedures, based on the department's goals and objectives.

However, if we limit others from sharing their input, that can create bottlenecks, which will have a direct impact on productivity– and productivity has a direct impact on profit.

If team members are allowed to mentally navigate to their own conclusions, and if the leadership team and coworkers throughout an organization are receptive to one another's thoughts and ideas, a collaborative environment is created, and our combined efforts to achieve the desired outcomes are more effective.

Interpersonal skills have proven to be a really good asset for me personally. When I was working as a department manager in corporate America, being able to display empathy for my employees was really important. Empathy is an interpersonal skill.

My goal in a leadership role in corporate America was to establish rapport with both employees and customers. Here's an example:

Our organization had just put new contracts in place, and I could easily see that my client was distressed over it. It wasn't unusual for my company to do that as it had to do with customer compliance with the business initiatives that were important to our organization.

Granted, every time we made these contract changes, it required our customers to reassess how they were promoting our product and services, and often it would have a financial impact as well.

Seeing the expression on my customer's face, I immediately displayed empathy – letting him know that I understood what he was experiencing. I got that he would have to make some financial adjustments in order to meet our corporation's business needs. So I listened very intently to understand the issues and challenges he was facing, and how challenging it might be for him to rearrange his own business in order to be in alignment with our company.

As I patiently and intently listened to him speak, I was able to understand exactly what his concerns were. I also understood what our new company policies and procedures were as it pertained to this contract change.

After hearing him out, I figured out how we could address his concerns and ended up helping him rearrange the structure of his business to be able to comply with our corporate needs. In doing so, I established a relationship and a friendship that was built on trust, transparency, and, of course, meeting my client where he was.

As I continued to utilize my interpersonal skills with this particular client, I shared the experience with my staff, to leverage it as a coaching opportunity. When the corporation would make these changes, there was always a reason behind them and they were adopted to improve our business. But initially they often had a negative impact on our customers because the new contracts and requirements were forced upon them without their consent.

I knew we had to tread cautiously and carefully in presenting this new contract to many of our clients. I coached my staff to really listen to our clients' concerns, with the intent of understanding them rather than shooting them down. I asked them to become acutely aware of what the clients would need to be able to successfully make the transition to the new contract with our company.

We learned from our clients that the timing would make a big difference. Because we were in communication with other departments, we were able to work together as a team to make minor adjustments based on what was important to the clients. All in all, we were able to make something very positive out of that daunting new contract and we found ways to serve our clients, helping them to successfully navigate through the transition. By doing so, we were able to both strengthen our relationships with the clients and meet and exceed our company's objectives.

Conflict Between Departments

In my previous experiences in the corporate environment, my primary responsibility was generating sales revenue for the companies that employed me. It wasn't unusual for our marketing and sales teams to clash. Earlier in my career, I didn't quite understand it. Marketing's primary responsibility was to create a brand message, increasing awareness of our product and services. They had initiatives and goals they had to accomplish.

In sales, our job was to generate revenue based on their marketing initiatives. If, by chance, we were struggling to meet our sales objectives, quite often we would be sitting around a table in the conference room, and sales department people would be pointing fingers, blaming marketing for their performance because *"the branding message was not as defined as it needed to be."*

Marketing was pointing fingers at sales, telling them the branding was perfect and that they just needed to do a better job of delivering the message.

It was us against them and I realized fairly early in my career that businesses' different departments don't stand alone, rather, they're interdependent, meaning, marketing needs sales, sales needs marketing, everyone needs accounting, operations, and so on and so on. We have to work together.

However, in many organizations the different departments are working *against* each other. This brings me right back to social skills. With the ability to manage relationships, even if there is a conflict, even if we do not see eye-to-eye, we don't need to allow those situations to tear us apart.

Instead, we can use clear thinking, we can use strategy, we can find processes to work together, and we can use our social skills and emotional intelligence to set our differences aside. We all have goals to accomplish for the betterment of the organization.

If, by chance, I disagreed on how to accomplish those goals, I learned to humble myself with a larger goal of resolving our differences – a positive outcome. My thought was that maybe I could be a better listener to understand another person's viewpoint, and by doing so, improve the opportunity for all of us to work together cohesively.

I wanted to understand the challenges of other departments as they pertained to accomplishing a given goal or objective. By being open to learning about another perspective, I was able to meet others where they were, so much so, that I could put differences aside so we could increase rapport with each other and build enough common ground where we may even be able to make compromises to work together in a united fashion. I sometimes chose to "take one for the team," such as giving up something our department wanted for the betterment of the overall organization.

Often, when leaders neglect to listen and learn, it has a negative domino effect on the whole company. In my mind, we all work for the same organization, but I've borne witness to managers who had issues with different departments and would complain about them to anyone who would listen – oth-

er department heads, peer groups, even their own staff. The
other managers would do the same and this, quite often, would
cultivate an "us against them" mentality which did not benefit
themselves, their departments, or the company as a whole.

This all-too-common dynamic creates what I call a **silo effect. This is when** all of these departments are working in
their own separate silos rather than working *together*, when
they actually need to coordinate and work with each other in
order for the organization to be successful.

Some companies get so stuck in this pattern, that at times
people develop outright hatred for their coworkers which, in
turn, creates systemic issues within the company and adversely
impacts their ability to maintain internal control, which interferes with the ability to serve clients and customers. If we cannot take care of each other in our own workplace, chances are
it will have a negative impact on our ability to take care of the
external customer. We call that "internal customer service."

Internal Customer Service

One could say that the internal customer – the person who
is sitting right next to you, in the next office, or down the hall –
is equally, if not more important, than the external customer.
This means that if we cannot look out for each other and address
our internal issues, if we cannot work through disagreements,
if we cannot build rapport and solid working relationships with
one another, chances are we're having a negative impact on our
end users, and we cannot see the forest for the trees.

As a whole, I am encouraging you to break out of your own "silo" as well as any departmental silo by leveraging social skills, focusing on self-awareness, increasing your social awareness, and maintaining a level of self-management. With one interaction, one engagement at a time, you can increase your emotional intelligence and your understanding of yourself and your decisions, and be able to leverage a positive influence on those around you.

Seeing how you impact others is always a good way to measure results!

Interpersonal Skills in a Leadership Role

Interpersonal skills are integral to management skills. They are what allow you to display empathy to your staff members.

For a leader, interpersonal skills are *crucial*. They are what allow you to establish trust with your staff and within your organization.

I'll often ask leaders, "Is trust a given, or is trust earned?"

The fact of the matter is, it is very subjective. I encourage leaders to trust their employees first. Now, that may be turning the leadership scale upside down but I've found throughout my business career that when I offer my employees my trust at the outset, they communicate with me more freely, even about their own shortcomings and mistakes at an earlier stage, if in fact, they have them. They appreciate and value our relationship, because I demonstrate early on that I trust them and I also create an environment where it's okay to make a mistake.

Of course, we want to manage this appropriately. We allow for mistakes, they're unavoidable. Our new hires will make mistakes, but if they hide those mistakes, it creates a lot more problems than the mistakes themselves. If they make the same mistakes over and over, for an extended period of time, we may need to call upon additional interpersonal skills to determine the cause, and find a solution. Maybe they misunderstood part of their training, or maybe we need to get them more aligned with the company vision and mission. What is your strategy for guiding your staff to achieve the goals of your department or your company?

As a leader, your team, as well as the entire organization, is relying on you. Interpersonal skills in a leadership role are so important because they give you the ability to influence others, and inspire them. Employees like to be led. They don't often like to be told what to do, but they do like to be led and guided toward a successful outcome.

Interpersonal skills allow you to be people-focused. Yes, we're all there to do a job, and that's very important – the job must be done. Being people-focused means focusing on what's important to your people so you can foster collaboration, flexibility, and the motivation to perform their job as well as they can to achieve the desired results. Without it, you're likely to see your staff operating counter to successful outcomes.

So, being people-focused is crucial. Investing in your people is investing in human capital– *your greatest asset.*

Of course, if I'm hiring you to do a job, I expect you to do the job. That doesn't change. However, when employees realize I genuinely care about them, that I'm willing to listen to them, and that I'm protecting them from undo pressure because I put their wellbeing first whenever possible, they almost always do their job exceedingly well.

When organizations as a whole are able to do that, for the most part, they find there's no need to micromanage the employees they have, and they also have less turnover. When you're people-focused, your employees naturally feel valued, so you don't have to worry about them being productive and doing their jobs.

Research and statistics show that the companies who are game to invest in their people, their human capital, are more productive and profitable overall. Their staff members are happier. It actually reduces absenteeism. There's less "drama" within the organization.

It's also a very proactive leadership and management style. By anticipating issues and challenges that your employees may encounter, if you do this properly and consistently, the payback is awesome for your organization in a variety of different ways. More importantly, if you want your employees to consistently focus on your customers, I highly encourage you to focus on them. As we spend more time developing our employees and doing our best to meet their needs – for approval and recognition, an ergonomic workspace, whatever it is – this becomes a transferable skill that they will use to meet the needs of customers.

The Importance of Embracing Change

Change is inevitable. As a leader, you must understand the importance of embracing change.

Even more importantly, you must be able to model the ability to embrace change for the sake of your employees, as well as to show empathy for them having to go through changes, especially unexpected ones.

As a leader, I've actually implemented change with our staff and all the folks with whom we were interacting. What I've noticed is that it can be similar to going through the grief process.

There's often a very emotional response. If your staff or customers did not agree with a change initially, or if change is being imposed upon them, the first reaction may be shock. They may be thinking, *What the heck are they doing?*

They may go into denial that change is at hand, or deny that they will ever accept it. Whether an employee or a customer, they may decide, *There is no way I'm going to accept this new policy or procedure.*

The next emotional response is frustration that can escalate to outright anger.

They've been personally impacted by a change or changes, and when they realize things are not going to go back to the way they were, they may feel helpless and even transition into a state of depression.

This is a very volatile state because a change or changes have occurred, more than likely we are not going backwards, and people can get stuck in their resistance to the change. This could last for a period of time.

However, it's possible to navigate through that state of depression fairly quickly. For example, when they recognize the negative effects weren't nearly as bad as they imagined. Even better, if they have curiosity, they can more easily move into the acceptance stage. When they see the positive sides of a change, they can get enthusiastic about it, to the point where they're actually embracing it and, finally, committing to help implement it.

Quite often, as a leader, you're exposed to changes earlier and more frequently than your staff members are. As leaders, we typically go through the same set of emotions in response to change. So we need to be consciously aware that the people we're responsible for are going to go through the exact same process, and we may need to coach them through it.

Once we ourselves have accepted a change, we may judge an employee's lack of being on board, lack of engagement or participation, or actively resisting a change, as that person *"not being a team player."*

But the fact of the matter is, they're simply going through their own emotional response.

Vulnerability is a Sign of Strength

This brings me to the next level of interpersonal skills: the importance of vulnerability. Vulnerability is a very interesting topic to me, because, like so many people, I was taught from a young age that vulnerability is a sign of weakness.

The fact of the matter is **vulnerability is a sign of strength**.

When we're able to reveal our own vulnerabilities, especially as leaders, it actually engages people. It requires a healthy sense of self-confidence, and demonstrates transparency and trustworthiness. It also opens the door to more interaction.

You don't want to leave yourself completely exposed but a healthy, appropriate amount of vulnerability can turn a potentially negative interaction into a positive engagement, because you're communicating to your employees that you too are human. This makes you relatable and strengthens your working relationship, which ultimately translates into increased productivity and profit.

So, I encourage all leaders, employees, and anyone else to embrace their own vulnerability.

My simple question again, *Is trust a given, or is trust earned?*

I've found that, as a leader, as I give my trust to my staff and others, I receive the same in return. Of course, we want to safeguard ourselves to make sure we're not being exploited or allowing others to take advantage of us. I do understand that, to a degree.

I also understand the importance of communicating trust to employees first. It often is what allows me to truly trust them going forward, because if they know I trust them, they will be transparent with me. They will even share with me when they're facing challenges, allowing me to offer my perspective because they trust me to have their best interests at heart.

This not only applies to our business lives, but to our personal lives as well. So, I encourage leaders to embrace trust, embrace vulnerability, and embrace change. These are powerful interpersonal skills that will encourage the same skills within your team, and you will all be able to expect great things to happen.

CHAPTER 14:
HAVING DIFFICULT
CONVERSATIONS

Being able to communicate directly and assertively is important. Assertive communication is that sweet spot between aggressive and passive-aggressive or passive. Just because you can tell people what you think and what's on your mind, doesn't mean you're doing it in an effective way. If you do that without measuring impact, chances are you can easily offend someone, albeit unintentionally.

Being direct doesn't always mean you're doing it in the "emotional intelligence way." If you're communicating directly with your audience or your team members or others, and if they feel like they have been taken advantage of, like they've been hit in the face by a verbal assault, then chances are you're not practicing Emotional Intelligence.

The ability to have a difficult conversation is a valuable skill. One that encourages you to listen objectively and to take in all sides of a story, all perspectives. One that requires you to answer questions, questions upon questions, to be strategic, to dig deeper, to gain a better understanding of the situation, as well as the people involved.

Difficult Conversations with a Boss or Supervisor

When I was working for Randy, I noticed he was the type of leader who had a black-and-white way of thinking. He always stuck to the rules, policies, and procedures. It was his style of leadership and it seemed to be very effective.

However, the impact of that leadership style began to weigh on my staff. I began to hear complaints like, "Why can't we adjust the policy to accommodate the needs of our customers and the needs of our workforce?"

Our policies and procedures are extremely important in this area of the business but often, as leaders, we need to review policies and perhaps adjust them based on a new environment and/or the culture of our people.

As this dialogue with my direct reports continued, they began to build a very compelling case for working remotely, which encouraged me to have a difficult conversation with my leader. After doing my research to understand why my manager believed so strongly in the core principle of not working remotely, I began to understand the areas of opportunity in accommodating my staff, such as being able to travel within a matter of minutes from home to their first customer, as opposed to first driving into the office and then going back out to their geographically-assigned area to take care of these customers.

As I gathered my facts and my data, I built up the courage to have a conversation with the boss to ask a very simple question, "Why can we not make an adjustment? Why can we not accommodate the needs of our employees? It would have a positive impact on their morale."

That moment took a lot of courage and discipline on my part, to really listen objectively to what my boss wanted to communicate. More importantly, I did not want to offend him or challenge his authority.

Yet, I had a responsibility to my staff to bring up this conversation that could perhaps make things better for them. As I was able to interact with my boss this way, with transparency about my reasoning and my sincere motivation to help my staff, and also listen objectively to why these policies were important to him, I was able to gain more of his trust.

He had a fear, and that fear was that the employees would no longer be accountable and responsible. But the team I had grown and developed were actually quite disciplined and quite focused. So we were able to achieve a happy medium. He gave me the autonomy to try out this remote work experience and follow-up with him on a regular basis to see what type of progress we were making.

The fact of the matter is, it takes courage to have these types of conversations, and to do it well, it takes listening to different sides of a topic or issue objectively. But if we're going to move business forward, at times we do have to challenge the status quo. So, I'm encouraging all of you to do the same when you deem it necessary.

Having difficult conversations isn't easy. However, when we do have difficult conversations with people who have more authority, we position ourselves to become better leaders ourselves, and we can expect great things to happen.

Difficult Conversations with Customers

At Nextel Communications, I was the Indirect Account Manager. Part of my responsibility was to post the new promotions we were focusing on each month. I was responsible for about 40 different accounts, and the way I went about my business was to email them about the promotion a week or so prior to the actual promotion date.

Once they received these promotions, they could simply print out the labels, the new pricing models, and post them throughout their office for the new promotion.

Fast forward, after the beginning of the new month, I would visit all my dealers at their stores to ensure they had the proper pricing promotions on display. That was my responsibility. I noticed in one of my stores, they still had the old promo.

I immediately went over to the sales rep and asked, "Why are you promoting last month's activity?"

His immediate response was, "Richard, we didn't receive an email. We had no idea the promotions had changed."

I said, "Of course you guys did. I sent it out to all of your stores."

I got a follow-up call from his boss who began to chew me out. "What the heck is going on? All of the stores we have here in the Houston market, they're all promoting the old pricing. Why didn't you send us the new pricing?"

I interrupted him. "Of course I sent you the new prices, as I always do with all my clients. Why didn't you receive it? Why aren't you displaying it?"

He hung up and, very distressed, he immediately called my boss to complain about my lack of follow-through, at least from his perspective.

I immediately returned to the office to have a conversation with my boss, who asked me one simple question: "Is there anything you could have done better?"

I paused for a moment; I was reluctant to reply. "Well, once I sent that email, I could have called them to validate they actually received the new promotion. However, I did not have to do that with any of my other clients but, apparently, I could have done that for these folks."

Having difficult conversations with a customer is not easy. The fact of the matter was that I had followed the protocol given to me by my leaders. However, in this situation, the customer was still without the proper information that they needed in order for them to be successful.

So having that difficult conversation with the customer was very hard. Even more difficult was having the conversation with my boss to figure out what I could have done differently to improve that customer's experience, which was to do something different for them next time because it was the right thing to do.

Now, you may feel differently, but in order to meet our customer's needs, we may have to make an adjustment, even if it means extra work for us. One size does not fit all. I encourage you to embrace having difficult conversations with your customers, then expect great things to happen.

Difficult Conversations with Peers

Back in 2008, I had the opportunity to take over for a leader at my job. When this position was described to me, I realized the leader I was taking over for had managed his staff through fear. The interesting thing was that his communication and leadership style was the same as how his leader had managed him.

I remember having a conversation with his boss later at his condo that was shocking to me. He said, "Richard, when I go in to work, my goal is to be like a bull in a China cabinet. I want to disrupt the employees. I want them to literally 'shit the bed.'"

The gentleman who replaced him mimicked his leadership style and morale was low.

People were scared and wary of their jobs. They were afraid to report issues and challenges they were encountering, all because of this individual's intimidating leadership style.

So, upon taking this assignment, I began to ask questions. "What is it you would like for me to do?"

My current boss said, "Just do what you do."

I told him that to "do what I do" means that I sit down and listen to the employees. I find out what challenges or barriers they face. After that, I have awkward conversations with my boss to let him or her know what the issues are.

Interestingly, my new boss in the interim was the same gentleman who had the concept of being a bull in a China cabinet. As I sat down to speak with my new manager, I said, "Listen, I'm honored to take on this role and responsibility, but the way you interact and engage with people will undermine what I've been asked to do here.

"Will you allow me to do my job to the best of my ability in order to bring peace and calm to the work environment?"

He said, "Richard, that is what needs to be done. How you get it done is up to you."

So that created an opportunity to have a conversation with my peer, the gentleman whom I was temporarily replacing. Ironically, his name was Richard as well and he was in the same office while I was managing his team. It was a very awkward situation. We were working inside the same office, yet I had responsibility for his team while he worked on another project.

One day, I built up the courage to have a conversation with him. My goal was to help him, to encourage him to be the best leader he could possibly be. I knew he had it within himself, and I encouraged him to add what was missing.

I suggested that he show his people that he actually cares. Yes, they still have goals and responsibilities and they need to meet their objectives. But the way to have a conversation with an employee is NOT to intimidate them with, "Do this or else!"

That's a scare tactic that will only cause them to withdraw. It contributes to their inability to make the connections they need to make to get past the roadblocks and barriers they face because they're scared. And, ultimately, they will lose respect for you because of the way you were communicating with them.

I continued a dialogue with Richard, sharing with him how my leadership style was more embracing of the employees and showing them empathy. It was about encouraging these people to do what we hired them to do, rather than berate them. We're paying them a good amount and we want them to act like responsible adults, so we have to show that we respect them. We have to show them that we care about them, and in doing so, they will become more aligned with the company goals and objectives.

I wanted him to display some vulnerability and at least admit there's a more delicate way of getting people to do their jobs. He said it wasn't his skillset. But it was mine, and I demonstrated a different way of leading. I was able to take the strategic thoughts he communicated to me and deliver them in a way where it was received favorably by the team.

He had to build up the muscle and gain confidence to be able to communicate in a new way. So he said, "Okay, I'm not going to accuse anyone about why they aren't doing their job. I'm going to ask them, 'Could you please help me?' I'm going to ask, 'How did you approach this? What was your thought behind this? How did you come to this conclusion?'"

He told me he gained some understanding on how they were thinking and perhaps now he could respond appropriately, or coach and guide them accordingly, as opposed to accusing them.

"But," he said, "they're doing a terrible job, and their defenses come up. They won't talk. They just sit there and take it."

He was realizing that losing his temper didn't work for him, and that's what his leader was doing to him. His leader, whom he had emulated, was known for the "swoop and poop."

I learned this term working for this group. Our leader was in Denver, while we were in Albuquerque, and he would fly into Albuquerque and sh-- all over everything. Our group would be scared to death as he bawled them out, "You're not doing this! You need to fix this! You need to fix that!"

Then he would get back on a plane back to Denver.

Anyhow, Richard never did end up supervising that group again, the damage had been done, but he had learned that there are more effective ways to communicate with staff than "swooping and pooping."

Having difficult conversations with your peers can be challenging, but if you're grounded in an intention of helping them to be their best, you'll be amazed at what you can accomplish. Again, expect great things to happen!

Difficult Conversations with Direct Reports

There was a gentleman I used to manage a few years ago and we'll call him Simon. He was very engaging and had a great personality. He was a "social butterfly."

What he lacked was follow through. He lacked customer focus. I started to receive calls from some of his customers.

I responded immediately by calling him into the office to address the issue, to get a level of understanding of why and how he had fallen short of the customers' expectations.

He shared with me how busy he had been. He even began to justify his behavior to me, that he had actually called the customer back on several occasions and they had simply misinterpreted his overtures.

At the end of this first conversation, I encouraged him to make sure that he followed through, that he dotted his I's and crossed his T's to make sure he followed up with the clients according to their expectations.

A week later I received a phone call from my boss asking me what in the heck is going on with Simon because he too was starting to receive complaints about his lack of follow through and carrying out the initiatives requested by the customers, as well as our business. He asked me to have a conversation with him. I told my boss, "I did. I already had a conversation with Simon and he had agreed this was not going to continue."

So, I called Simon into the office once again for a better understanding of where he was misinterpreting the expectations and to help him gain clarity.

We decided to call the customer to verify exactly what he expected, which we did. We committed that we would follow through and that I would be personally involved to ensure Simon fulfilled his obligation. He immediately addressed the issue and fixed it.

However, two weeks later, my boss received another telephone call complaining about Simon and his lack of follow through. My boss asked me a very simple question: "Richard, are you going to allow the lack of Simon's follow through cost you, your job?"

I said, "Of course not."

I had yet another conversation with Simon, documenting his lack of follow through with the customers, and I placed him on a written and verbal warning.

Quite often we, as managers, would like to take our employees and what they say at face value. In most cases throughout my career, that has been the mindset behind my leadership style. I trusted them, so they trusted me, but there were occasions when individuals did not follow up or do what they were supposed to do.

Following up with your employees, nipping any miscommunications in the bud, and addressing their concerns are all important parts of nurturing them, counseling them, and helping them grow. Of course, if they're not following processes, you should coach them on how to be better as this will only help your employees to achieve their own positive desired outcomes.

IN CONCLUSION:
EXPECT GREAT THINGS
TO HAPPEN

By working with the five principles, you will develop the skills it takes to be a "business athlete." With practice, practice, and more practice, applying these principles day to day, you can duplicate and even surpass the results achieved by highly effective business professionals.

My goal with this book was to provide, in a non-threatening way, a clear blueprint for readers to advance their own careers while having a positive impact in the lives of others. My hope is that you will take actionable steps to intentionally and purposefully encourage, motivate, listen to, empathize with, and embrace the individuals in your spheres of influence – employees, supervisors, peers, clients, friends, and family.

As a leader, you have a responsibility and you need to be able to take it seriously. It's a leader's job to provide a healthy productive work environment in which everyone is able to thrive and be the best version of themselves, regardless of their current position.

This is not a one-size-fits-all approach. Flexibility and adaptability are your best friends to adjust your style to accommodate those you lead. To support each individual and meet them where they are means taking the time to understand their needs, their wants, their goals, their objectives, and to help fulfill them. Often that requires improving your active listening skills.

I want you to be a courageous leader. To implement these strategies takes courage, overcoming your own fears and biases so you can redefine what a great leader is, for these times, as well as the future. What I'm asking you to do is challenge the status quo and to genuinely care about your most important asset: the people who work at your organization.

To propel your own career, you must invest in others. This requires self-sacrifice for the betterment of your team or group or company, whomever you're leading. By doing that, you will organically rise to the level of being a great leader, like the other positive change agents and influencers who become respected, even legendary, in their own time.

When you develop, coach, and mentor the people who work for you, they learn through their interactions with you. In this way, you will be able to positively impact lives all across the world, one interaction at a time – allowing a ripple effect to create the positive change we all aspire to be.

Expect great things to happen!

APPENDIX

https://rdmmanagementgroup.com/bookstore

https://rdmmanagementgroup.com/, Company Website

https://rdm.mykajabi.com/unconsciousbias - On-demand Course Unconscious Bias $$$

https://rdm.mykajabi.com/unconsciousbias

https://rdm.mykajabi.com/engaginginhealthyconflict - On-demand Course Engaging In Healthy Conflict $$$

https://rdm.mykajabi.com/levelup - On-demand Course Management Course (Level -Up) $$$$

ExpectGreatThingsToHappen.com, - eBook free

https://rdmmanagementgroup.com/assessments - Assessment offerings $$$

https://rdmmanagementgroup.com/ken-blanchard - Blanchard Partner Network offerings $$$$

https://rdmmanagementgroup.com/the-empowerment-series - Motivational Stories Free Download

https://rdmmanagementgroup.com/courses-offered - Training Offerings by RDM Management Group

REFERENCES

Emotional Intelligence 2.0 by Travis Bradberry and Jean Greaves

Mindset: The New Psychology of Success by Carol Dweck

Principles: by Ray Dalio

AUTHOR BIO

Richard D. Marks is the owner of RDM Management Group. Established in 2014, RDM is a training company which specializes in professional development, sales, and leadership training in both the public and private sector.

Richard's expertise includes leading large and small organizations, developing teams to achieve high performance levels, rebuilding teams after they've been exposed to toxic leadership, and downsizing teams based on market conditions and business objectives.

Richard trains business teams and leaders on over forty professional development topics that include Leadership Training, Diversity and Inclusion, Unconscious Bias, Time Management, Managing a Hybrid Workforce, Managing Remotely, Engaging in Healthy Conflict, Conflict Resolution, Effective Communication, Strategic Thinking, Tactical Execution, Coaching, Counseling and Mentoring, Change Management, and Cultural and Emotional Intelligence.

Richard is a U.S. Army Veteran with thirty years of experience working in corporate America, ranging from individual contributor to mid-level manager to senior leadership. These experiences helped make him a relatable and authentic Servant Leader, Facilitator, Coach, Business Athlete, and Keynote Speaker.

Richard is the author of the inspirational CDs, *The Empowerment Series Volume I & II* and author of the on-demand courses, *Engaging in Healthy Conflict, Unconscious Bias, Level-Up Management*, and *Business Sales Course*.

Richard lives by two mantras which guide him each day: *"Expect Great Things to Happen"* and *"Positively Impacting the World, One Training at a Time."*